Tribes of Israel

Exploring the History, Culture, and Legacy of the Israelite Tribes

IBL Press

Table of Contents

Prologue

In the annals of ancient history, amid the sands of time and the whispers of tradition, the narrative of the 12 tribes of Israel stands as a testament to the enduring legacy of a people bound by blood, faith, and destiny. Rooted in the sacred texts of the Hebrew Bible, the story of these tribes transcends mere historical accountancy; it embodies the essence of identity, inheritance, and covenant.

At the heart of this narrative lies the patriarch Jacob, whose life journey unfolds within the pages of Genesis, the book of beginnings. Jacob, whose name was later changed to Israel, fathered twelve sons, each destined to become the progenitor of a distinct tribe, forging the foundation upon which the nation of Israel would be built.

The genesis of the 12 tribes is woven into the fabric of Jacob's life, marked by familial strife, divine encounters, and providential blessings. From the rivalry between Jacob's wives, Leah and Rachel, to the jealousy and betrayal that culminated in the sale of Joseph into slavery, the saga of the tribes is imbued with the complexities of human relationships and the divine orchestration of history.

As Jacob lay on his deathbed, he summoned his sons to impart his final blessings upon them, prophetically delineating their respective destinies and roles within the emerging nation. These blessings, recorded in Genesis 49, offer a glimpse into the character and calling of each tribe, foretelling their strengths, weaknesses, and contributions to the collective tapestry of Israel's identity.

The journey of the 12 tribes did not end with the passing of their patriarch. Rather, it unfolded across the landscape of ancient Canaan, as the descendants of Jacob multiplied and established themselves as a distinct people within the land promised to their forefathers. Led by tribal chieftains and guided by divine providence, they navigated the trials of wilderness wanderings, territorial conflicts, and cycles of apostasy and redemption.

The concept of the 12 tribes of Israel transcends mere genealogy or geopolitical organization; it embodies a spiritual inheritance, a covenantal bond between a chosen people and their God. From the shores of the Red Sea to the heights of Mount Sinai, from the fertile valleys of Ephraim to the desolate wilderness of Dan, the tribes of Israel bore witness to the faithfulness of Yahweh and the enduring promise of a land flowing with milk and honey.

In the pages that follow, we embark on a journey of exploration and discovery, tracing the footsteps of the 12 tribes through the annals of history and legend. From their origins in the tents of Jacob to their dispersion among the nations, we seek to unravel the mysteries of their identity, the complexities of their tribal dynamics, and the enduring significance of their legacy in the tapestry of human history.

Join us as we delve into the rich tapestry of the 12 tribes of Israel, where the echoes of ancient prophecy meet the rhythms of divine providence, and where the covenantal bonds of faith and heritage continue to shape the destiny of a people called by name, beloved by their God.

Chapter 1: Story of Jacob

In the annals of ancient Hebrew scripture, the Book of Genesis serves as the foundational narrative of the Israelite people, chronicling the lives, struggles, and triumphs of their patriarchs and matriarchs. At the heart of this narrative lies the story of Jacob, who, through divine providence and human frailty, fathered twelve sons, each destined to become the progenitor of a distinct tribe, thus laying the groundwork for the emergence of the nation of Israel.

Birth:

Jacob and his twin brother, Esau, entered the world amidst a prophecy of divine revelation, their birth heralded by a tumultuous struggle within their mother's womb. Rebecca, their mother, sought guidance from the Almighty when she felt the turmoil within her, and she received a revelation that the twins she carried would be locked in perpetual conflict, destined to become the progenitors of two distinct nations. This prophecy foretold a future where the younger would surpass the elder, a theme that would echo throughout their lives and shape the course of history.

When the moment of birth arrived, Esau emerged first, his body covered in a thick mantle of red hair, earning him the name Esau, which means "hairy" in Hebrew. In a striking scene, Jacob followed, clutching onto his brother's heel as if seeking to assert his presence from the very moment of his birth. Thus, the twins were named Esau and Jacob, with Jacob's name carrying the connotation of "heel-catcher" or "supplanter," hinting at the role he would play in the unfolding drama of their lives.

From their earliest days, Esau and Jacob displayed contrasting temperaments and pursuits. Esau, the elder, was depicted as a skilled hunter, a man of the outdoors, while Jacob was described as a more tranquil figure, content to dwell in the

7

shelter of tents. Their differing personalities were mirrored in the attitudes of their parents: Isaac, their father, favored Esau for his prowess in the hunt, while Rebecca, their mother, harbored a special affection for Jacob.

This familial dynamic set the stage for a series of events that would shape the destiny of the twin brothers and their descendants. As they matured, their paths diverged ever further, leading to conflicts, betrayals, and ultimately, reconciliation. Yet, even in the midst of their struggles, the divine hand of providence could be discerned, guiding their steps and fulfilling the prophecy uttered at their birth.

The story of Esau and Jacob serves as a microcosm of the larger narrative of the twelve tribes of Israel, highlighting themes of sibling rivalry, divine favor, and the tension between destiny and human agency. In their tale, we find echoes of the struggles and triumphs that characterize the human condition, reminding us that even in the midst of conflict and uncertainty, the promise of redemption and reconciliation shines bright.

Blessing of Isaac:

In the pages of Genesis, a poignant narrative unfolds, chronicling the intricate web of familial relationships and divine intervention that shaped the destiny of the twelve tribes of Israel. Among the many stories that punctuate this epic saga, the account of Esau and Jacob stands as a testament to the complexities of human nature, the consequences of deceit, and the sovereignty of divine providence.

Genesis 25:29–34 unveils a pivotal moment in the lives of the twin brothers, Esau and Jacob. Famished from his outdoor pursuits, Esau returns to his brother's tent, craving sustenance. In a moment of vulnerability, he beseeches Jacob for a portion of the stew that simmers tantalizingly before him. This humble request sets in motion a chain of events that will reverberate throughout generations to come.

Seizing upon his brother's hunger and desperation, Jacob proposes a fateful bargain: a bowl of stew in exchange for Esau's birthright—the sacred inheritance and privileges reserved for the firstborn son. In a moment of weakness, Esau acquiesces, trading his birthright for a fleeting taste of sustenance, thus sealing his fate and altering the course of their family's history.

As time passes, the aging patriarch Isaac, now blind and uncertain of his days, prepares to bestow his blessings upon his eldest son, Esau. Unbeknownst to him, Rebecca, his wife, overhears his intentions and recognizes the opportunity for her favored son, Jacob, to receive the blessings instead. Drawing upon her prophetic insight, Rebecca orchestrates a deceptive scheme to ensure Jacob's ascension to the birthright blessings that rightfully belong to Esau.

Disguised in Esau's garments and adorned with goatskins to mimic his brother's hairy skin, Jacob enters his father's presence, ready to perpetrate the ruse. Isaac, initially suspicious, is ultimately convinced by Jacob's subterfuge and bestows upon him the blessings reserved for Esau. In a moment of revelation, Isaac acknowledges Jacob's divine favor, proclaiming, "Indeed, he will be blessed!"

Meanwhile, Esau returns from the hunt, only to discover the deception that has deprived him of his birthright and blessings. Consumed by grief and rage, he vows vengeance against his brother, prompting Rebecca to intervene once more, orchestrating Jacob's departure to her brother Laban's house in Haran until Esau's wrath subsides.

Jacob's ladder:

Amidst the journey from Luz to Haran, Jacob encounters a divine revelation that would shape the course of his destiny and that of his descendants—the vision of a ladder stretching from earth to heaven, adorned with ascending and descending angels. This celestial phenomenon, immortalized in popular culture as "Jacob's ladder," unfolds as a profound encounter with the divine.

In this mystical vision, Jacob hears the voice of God echoing from the pinnacle of the ladder, reiterating the blessings bestowed upon him and reaffirming the covenantal promises made to his forefathers. It is a moment of divine communion, where heaven and earth converge, and the transcendent realm is made manifest before mortal eyes.

According to Pirkei DeRabbi Eliezer,an aggadic-midrashic work on the Torah containing exegesis and retellings of biblical stories, the symbolism of the ladder extends beyond the confines of Jacob's immediate experience, pointing towards the future tribulations and triumphs of the Jewish people. Each angel ascending the ladder represents a successive exile endured by the Jewish nation—Babylonia, Persia, and Greece—marked by periods of subjugation and spiritual struggle. Yet, even as these exiles culminate in despair, the angel representing the final exile of Edom ascends ever higher, symbolizing the enduring power and resilience of God's chosen people.

In the light of dawn, Jacob awakens from his vision, his heart stirred by the promise of divine providence and redemption. He christens the place where he communed with God "Bethel," meaning "God's house," a testament to the sanctity of the encounter and the enduring presence of the divine in the midst of his earthly journey.

With renewed purpose and resolve, Jacob resumes his pilgrimage to Haran, bearing within him the echoes of his celestial vision and the assurance of God's guiding hand upon his life. In the footsteps of his ancestors, he traverses the wilderness of uncertainty, fortified by the promise that even amidst the trials and tribulations of exile, the ultimate redemption of his people is assured.

Marriages:

As Jacob journeyed to Haran, he encountered a scene familiar to those traversing the arid landscapes of the ancient world—a well surrounded by shepherds, gathering their flocks to quench their thirst. Among these shepherds was Laban's younger daughter, Rachel, a vision of beauty and grace who captured Jacob's heart upon their first meeting. Despite the years that had passed, Jacob, now 77 years old, found himself instantly drawn to Rachel, his first cousin, and desired to make her his wife.

Having spent a month in the company of his relatives, Jacob approached Laban, Rachel's father, with a proposal to marry her in exchange for seven years of labor. Laban, shrewd in his dealings, agreed to the arrangement, and Jacob willingly devoted himself to the labor of love, for the affection he held for Rachel made the years seem but a fleeting moment.

Yet, when the appointed time came for Jacob to claim his bride, Laban deceived him, substituting Rachel's older sister, Leah, veiled and disguised, as the bride. In the light of dawn, when the truth was revealed, Jacob confronted Laban, who justified his actions according to the customs of his land. However, Laban offered Rachel to Jacob as well, on the condition that he labor another seven years for her hand in marriage.

Thus, Jacob found himself bound to Laban's household for another cycle of labor, his love for Rachel undiminished despite the trials and deceptions he endured. In due time, Jacob wed Rachel, and his household expanded as Leah and Rachel bore him children, each son a testament to the enduring legacy of their forebears.

As years passed, Jacob, now in his 80s, experienced the joy of fatherhood, his household blessed with twelve children borne from the union of Rachel, Leah, and their handmaids. Yet, even amidst the blessings of fatherhood, Jacob's desire to return to his homeland burned within him, prompting him to seek Laban's permission to depart.

Laban, reluctant to part with his son-in-law, offered Jacob a portion of his flock as payment for his years of service. Jacob, wise in his negotiations, proposed a miraculous agreement—every spotted, speckled, and brown goat and sheep in Laban's flock would become his wages. Employing a stratagem involving striped rods placed in the watering holes, Jacob ensured the prosperity of his own flock, despite Laban's attempts at deception.

In the midst of these dealings, divine intervention was at work, as God revealed to Jacob the machinations of Laban and instructed him to return to his homeland. With his wives, children, and flocks in tow, Jacob embarked on his journey, leaving Laban behind and setting his sights on the land of his birth.

Yet, Laban, unwilling to let Jacob depart without a confrontation, pursued him for seven days, intent on reclaiming what he believed was rightfully his. In a dream, God warned Laban against speaking ill or good to Jacob, and upon their meeting, Laban confronted Jacob with accusations of deception and theft. Unaware of Rachel's theft of Laban's household idols, Jacob defended his innocence and parted ways with Laban, forging a pact of peace between them as they went their separate paths.

Thus, Jacob's sojourn in Haran came to an end, marked by trials, triumphs, and divine guidance, as he embarked on the next chapter of his journey—the return to the land of his forefathers, where his destiny awaited.

Journey back to Canaan:

As Jacob drew near to the land of Canaan, the specter of his past loomed large before him. News reached him that his brother Esau, with an entourage of 400 men, was approaching to meet him. Fearing the worst, Jacob beseeched God in fervent prayer, seeking guidance and protection in the face of imminent danger. In a gesture of appeasement, Jacob sent forth a tribute of flocks and herds to Esau, hoping to soften his brother's heart and avert conflict.

Under the cover of night, Jacob ferried his family and possessions across the ford Jabbok, a solitary figure grappling with his fears and uncertainties. There, in the stillness of the night, Jacob found himself engaged in a mysterious struggle with a divine being, wrestling until the break of dawn. In the throes of this ethereal encounter, the sinew of Jacob's thigh was touched, leaving him with a lasting reminder of his communion with the divine.

In the aftermath of the struggle, Jacob demanded a blessing from his enigmatic opponent, who proclaimed him "Israel," signifying his triumph in wrestling with the divine. Jacob, humbled and awed by the experience, named the place Penuel, declaring, "I have seen God face to face and lived."

The nature of Jacob's adversary remains shrouded in mystery, with interpretations varying widely—from a mere mortal to an angelic messenger or even God Himself. Yet, regardless of the being's identity, the encounter left an indelible mark on Jacob's soul, transforming him into Israel, a name synonymous with struggle, triumph, and divine favor.

As dawn broke, Jacob reunited with his wives and children, arranging them in a strategic order to greet Esau. Despite his apprehension, Esau's spirit was softened by Jacob's generous offerings, and their reunion was marked by tears of reconciliation and forgiveness.

Offering to accompany Jacob on his journey, Esau's offer was graciously declined, as Jacob deemed his children too young and tender for such a venture. Instead, Jacob proposed a future meeting at Mount Seir, a symbolic gesture with prophetic implications for the descendants of Jacob and Esau.

With Jacob's departure from Haran, the narrative unfolds with a series of trials and tribulations, including the abduction and rescue of his daughter Dinah, the tragic death of his beloved wife Rachel, and his eventual reunion with his father Isaac in Mamre. Amidst these trials, Jacob's faith and resilience are tested, yet his journey ultimately leads him back to the land of his forefathers, where his legacy as Israel, the one who struggled with God and prevailed, continues to reverberate through the annals of history.

Shechem:

Jacob then arrived in Shechem, where he bought a parcel of land, now identified as Joseph's Tomb. In Shechem, Jacob's daughter Dinah was kidnapped and raped by the ruler's son, who desired to marry the girl. Dinah's brothers, Simeon and Levi, agreed in Jacob's name to permit the marriage as long as all the men of Shechem first circumcised themselves, ostensibly to unite the children of Jacob in Abraham's covenant of familial harmony. On the third day after the circumcisions, when all the men of Shechem were still in pain, Simeon and Levi put them all to death by the sword and rescued their sister Dinah, and their brothers plundered the property, women, and children. Jacob condemned this act, saying: "You have brought trouble on me by making me a stench to the Canaanites and Perizzites, the people living in this land." He later rebuked his two sons for their anger in his deathbed blessing.

Bethel:

Jacob returned to Bethel, where he had another vision of blessing. Although the death of Rebecca, Jacob's mother, is not explicitly recorded in the Bible, Deborah, Rebecca's nurse, died and was buried at Bethel, at a place that Jacob calls Allon Bachuth, "Oak of Weepings" . According to the Midrash, the plural form of the word "weeping" indicates the double sorrow that Rebecca also died at this time.

In a somber turn of events, Jacob's journey is marked by profound loss and the enduring legacy of his beloved wife, Rachel. As Rachel nears the end of her pregnancy, tragedy strikes near the outskirts of Bethlehem.

Rachel goes into labor but tragically passes away while giving birth to her second son, Benjamin. Jacob is overcome with grief as he lays his beloved wife to rest, erecting a monument over her grave as a testament to their love and the enduring memory of Rachel. To this day, Rachel's Tomb stands as a revered site for pilgrims and prayers, a symbol of devotion and remembrance.

Amidst the mourning, Jacob finds himself faced with yet another challenge as his firstborn son, Reuben, commits a grave transgression by sleeping with Rachel's servant, Bilhah. Though Jacob's immediate response to this betrayal is not recorded, he later condemns Reuben for his actions in his deathbed blessing, highlighting the weight of responsibility that comes with the patriarchal mantle.

Despite the sorrow that shadows his journey, Jacob finds solace in the reunion with his father, Isaac, in Mamre. Together with his brother Esau, Jacob lays Isaac to rest in the Cave of the Patriarchs, a sacred site purchased by Abraham as a family burial plot. It is here, amidst the echoes of generations past, that Jacob confronts the complexities of family ties and the enduring legacy of his forefathers.

As Isaac's death marks the passing of an era, Jacob reflects on the intertwined destinies of his own lineage and that of his brother Esau. With the burial of Isaac, two genealogies of Esau's family emerge, shedding light on the intricate tapestry of ancestral connections. In a conservative interpretation, Jacob's acquisition of Esau's records at Isaac's burial symbolizes the convergence of family histories, intertwining the destinies of two brothers bound by blood and legacy.

As Jacob continues his journey, the echoes of loss and legacy reverberate through the corridors of time, shaping the destiny of his descendants and the unfolding narrative of the Israelite people.

In Hebron:

In the bustling land of Canaan, the house of Jacob found its abode in the ancient city of Hebron. Amidst the fertile pastures of Shechem and Dothan, Jacob's flocks grazed, tended by his sons and servants.

Among Jacob's offspring, none held a place as dear to his heart as Joseph, the son of his beloved Rachel. Adorned in a coat of many colors, Joseph stood out among his siblings, eliciting both envy and disdain from his half brothers. Joseph's dreams, foretelling a future where his family would bow before him, only stoked the flames of resentment within his brothers' hearts.

One fateful day, as Joseph's brothers tended to the flocks in Shechem, Jacob, eager for news, dispatched Joseph to bring back a report. Little did he know, it would be the last time he would see his cherished son within the walls of Hebron.

Upon Joseph's departure, tragedy struck. His brothers, consumed by jealousy and spite, concocted a deceitful plan. Presenting their father with Joseph's blood-stained coat, they spun a tale of a savage beast's attack, leaving Jacob to mourn the loss of his beloved son.

In anguish, Jacob lamented, tearing his garments and shrouding himself in mourning. Days passed, but the grief within the house of Jacob remained unassuaged, as the truth of Joseph's fate remained veiled in darkness.

Unbeknownst to Jacob, his sons' betrayal ran deep. They had not merely lost Joseph to the jaws of a wild beast; instead, they had callously sold him into slavery, condemning him to a fate unknown on a caravan bound for Egypt.

As the sun set over Hebron, the shadows of betrayal cast a long shadow over the house of Jacob, forever altering the course of their destiny.

Seven-year famine:

Years passed, marking two decades since the events that unfolded in Hebron. Across the Middle East, a devastating famine gripped the lands, its severity unmatched by any before it. For seven long years, nations faltered under its relentless grasp, their people languishing in despair.

Amidst this turmoil, whispers spread of a single kingdom untouched by the famine's ravages: Egypt. In the second year of the famine's onslaught, Israel, now aged around 130 years, summoned his ten sons born of Leah, Bilhah, and Zilpah. With a heavy heart, he instructed them to journey to Egypt and procure grain to sustain their family through the relentless drought. Only Benjamin, the youngest son born of Rachel, remained behind, sheltered by his father's protective embrace.

Upon their return from Egypt, laden with grain and laden with tales of their encounters, the brothers recounted their trials to their father. They spoke of accusations of espionage, of the imprisonment of Simeon, and of the demand to produce Benjamin as proof of their honesty. Israel's fury flared at their perceived folly, unable to fathom how they had revealed so much about their family to strangers.

As they unpacked their provisions, a startling discovery awaited them: the money they had used to purchase the grain still lay untouched in their sacks. Fear seized their hearts, compounded by their father's anguish over the loss of Joseph, Simeon, and now the potential jeopardy facing Benjamin.

Unbeknownst to them, Joseph, their long-lost brother, had orchestrated their plight from the shadows, secretly returning their payment. With their grain depleted, Israel urged his sons to return to Egypt for more provisions. This time, Judah stepped forth, pleading with his father to allow Benjamin to accompany them, fearing Egyptian reprisal and seeking to secure Simeon's release.

In a gesture of goodwill, Israel instructed his sons to bear gifts from their land and to return the doubled payment that had inexplicably found its way back to them. With a heavy heart and a prayer on his lips, Israel bid them farewell, resigned to whatever fate may befall them, uttering, "May God Almighty grant you mercy... And as for me, if I be bereaved of my children, I am bereaved".

Upon their return to Hebron, the sons of Jacob arrived with an impressive caravan of twenty additional donkeys laden with goods and supplies, along with Egyptian transport wagons. As their father emerged to greet them, they bore astonishing news: Joseph was alive and well, ruling as governor over all of Egypt, and he desired their household to relocate to Egypt. Israel was overcome with disbelief and awe, his heart faltering at the unimaginable revelation. Surveying the wagons, he exclaimed, "Joseph my son is still alive! I will go and see him before I die."

With their entire household of seventy souls and all their livestock, Israel embarked on the journey to Egypt. Along the way, they paused at Beersheba, where Israel offered sacrifices to Yahweh, seeking reassurance in prayer. Despite his apprehensions about leaving the land of his ancestors, God comforted him, promising that he would rise again, prosper, and behold his son Joseph, who would eventually lay him to rest.

As they drew near to Egypt, Israel sent his son Judah ahead to ascertain their destination. Directed to Goshen, they arrived after a journey of twenty-two years, where Israel was joyously reunited with Joseph. Embracing his long-lost son, they wept tears of happiness, and Israel declared, "Now I can die, since I have seen your face and know that you are still alive."

The time came for Joseph's family to meet the Pharaoh of Egypt. After Joseph prepared them for the audience, the brothers presented themselves before the Pharaoh, seeking permission to dwell in Egyptian lands. Impressed by Joseph's wisdom, the Pharaoh granted their request and even offered positions of authority to any skilled men among them. Finally, Israel was brought before the Pharaoh, who honored him out of respect for Joseph, treating him as an equal. Israel blessed the Pharaoh, and they conversed, with the Pharaoh expressing curiosity about Israel's age, which was then 130 years old.

Following the meeting, the families were settled in the land of Ramses, in the province of Goshen, where they prospered abundantly, even amidst the seven-year famine. The house of Jacob multiplied greatly, amassing wealth and possessions over the course of seventeen years.

Final days:

At the age of 147, Israel (Jacob) summoned his beloved son Joseph and made a heartfelt plea. He expressed his desire not to be buried in Egypt but to rest in the land of Canaan alongside his ancestors. Joseph solemnly swore to honor his father's wish. Soon after, Israel fell ill, his vision fading with age. When Joseph visited him, he brought his two sons, Ephraim and Manasseh, to receive their grandfather's blessing. Israel proclaimed them heirs to the inheritance of the house of Israel, treating them as if they were his own sons alongside Reuben and Simeon. With his right hand on Ephraim's head and his left on Manasseh's, Israel blessed Joseph. Yet, Joseph sought to place his father's right hand on Manasseh's head, the firstborn, but Israel insisted, declaring, "Truly, his younger brother shall be greater than he," echoing his own precedence over his older brother Esau. Israel then summoned all his sons to prophesy their blessings or curses in order of their birth.

Upon Israel's death, the entire family, along with the Egyptians, mourned for seventy days. His body was embalmed for forty days as Joseph made preparations for a grand ceremonial journey to Canaan. Leading Pharaoh's servants and the elders of both Israel and Egypt, they crossed the Jordan River to Atad, where they observed seven days of mourning. Their grief attracted the attention of the surrounding Canaanites, who remarked on the profound sorrow of the Egyptians. This location was named Abel Mizraim in honor of their mourning. Israel was laid to rest in the cave of Machpelah, the burial site purchased by Abraham from the Hittite Ephron.

Jacob, through his wives and concubines, fathered twelve sons: Reuben, Simeon, Levi, Judah, Dan, Naphtali, Gad, Asher, Issachar, Zebulun, Joseph, and Benjamin. Though the scene of Jacob mourning Joseph suggests the existence of daughters, details about them are scarce. Only one daughter, Dinah, is mentioned by name. Additionally, Jacob adopted Joseph's sons, Manasseh and Ephraim. The descendants of Jacob's sons formed the tribes of Israel after the Exodus, settling in the Promised Land.

Chapter 2: The Twelve Tribes of Israel

The Twelve Tribes of Israel hold a significant place in biblical history and tradition, representing the descendants of the twelve sons of Jacob, also known as Israel. According to the Book of Genesis, Jacob had twelve sons: Reuben, Simeon, Levi, Judah, Dan, Naphtali, Gad, Asher, Issachar, Zebulun, Joseph, and Benjamin.

Each of these sons became the progenitor of a tribe, with the exception of Joseph, whose two sons, Ephraim and Manasseh, each received a portion of the inheritance, bringing the total number of tribes to twelve. However, the tribe of Levi was designated as the priestly tribe and did not receive a territorial inheritance like the other tribes.

The Twelve Tribes of Israel played a crucial role in the history of the Israelites, from their time in Egypt under the oppression of Pharaoh to their conquest of the Promised Land under the leadership of Joshua. After settling in Canaan, each tribe received its allotted portion of land, as outlined in the Book of Joshua.

Throughout biblical narrative, the tribes are often depicted as distinct entities with unique characteristics and responsibilities. For example, Judah emerged as a dominant tribe, from which the line of kings, including King David and eventually Jesus, descended. The tribe of Levi was entrusted with the priestly duties, serving in the tabernacle and later in the temple in Jerusalem.

Over time, the Twelve Tribes of Israel faced various challenges, including conflicts with neighboring nations, internal strife, and periods of exile and dispersion. The Assyrian and Babylonian conquests resulted in the scattering of many Israelites, leading to the notion of the "Ten Lost Tribes."

Despite their dispersion, the legacy of the Twelve Tribes of Israel continues to resonate in Jewish tradition, shaping religious and cultural identity. In Christianity, the symbolism of the twelve tribes is often associated with the apostles and the foundation of the Church.

Below: Mosaic depicting the twelve tribes and their Hebrew names, with symbolic images:
- Asher: a tree
- Dan: Scales of justice
- Judah: Kinnor, cithara, and crown, symbolising King David
- Reuben: Mandrake (Genesis 30:14)
- Joseph: Palm tree and sheaves of wheat, symbolizing his time in Egypt
- Naphtali: gazelle (Genesis 49:21)
- Issachar: Sun, moon, and stars (1 Chronicles 12:32)
- Simeon: towers and walls of the city of Shechem
- Benjamin: jug, ladle, and fork
- Gad: tents, symbolizing their itinerancy as cattle herders
- Zebulun: ship, due to their bordering the Sea of Galilee and the Mediterranean
- Levi: Priestly breastplate

Land Allotment:

In the ancient division of the Land of Israel, as recounted in the Book of Joshua chapters 13 to 19, the territory was partitioned into twelve sections, each corresponding to one of the tribes of Israel. However, there were variations in the land allocation compared to the biblical tribes. The Tribe of Levi, designated for priestly duties, did not receive land but was entrusted with the administration of six Cities of Refuge and the sacred Temple in Jerusalem. Joseph's descendants, Ephraim and Manasseh, inherited their father's portion of land instead.

Therefore, the tribes that were allotted specific territories included Reuben, Simeon, Ephraim, Judah, Issachar, Zebulun, Dan, Naphtali, Gad, Asher, Manasseh, and Benjamin.

Below is a biblical map of the Twelve Tribes of Israel:

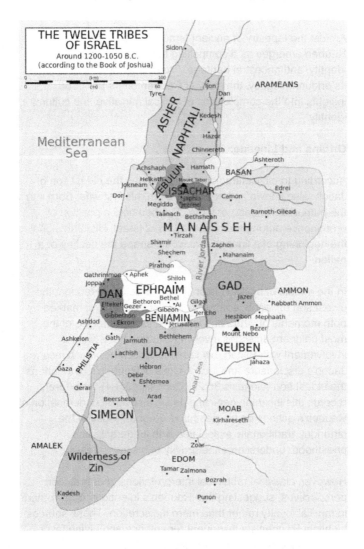

Chapter 3: The Tribe of Reuben

Amidst the tapestry of ancient Israelite history, the Tribe of Reuben emerges as a compelling testament to resilience, identity, and ancestral heritage. From its foundational roots to its enduring legacy, the story of Reuben offers profound insights into the complexities of biblical narrative and cultural identity.

Origins and Lineage:

According to biblical tradition, Reuben was the eldest son of Jacob, also known as Israel, and Leah, his first wife. Born into the patriarchal lineage of Israel, Reuben held a position of prominence among the twelve tribes of Israel. His birth signaled the beginning of a lineage that would shape the destiny of a nation.

In the annals of biblical history, the character of Reuben, the eldest son of Jacob, emerges as a complex figure, marked by both moments of virtue and lapses in judgment. One of the most poignant episodes involving Reuben is his sexual involvement with Bilhah, his father's concubine, which incurred Jacob's displeasure and led to a loss of Reuben's birthright as the eldest son (Genesis 35:22, Genesis 49:3-4). The Torah records this incident, depicting Jacob's severe condemnation of Reuben's actions on his deathbed. Reuben's loss of the birthright, traditionally associated with leadership and priesthood, underscores the gravity of his transgression.

However, classical rabbinical interpretations offer nuanced perspectives, suggesting that Reuben's intentions were rooted in familial loyalty rather than mere indiscretion. These sources highlight Reuben's subsequent repentance and divine favor, underscoring his status as the first penitent.

Despite his shortcomings, Reuben demonstrates moments of moral clarity and compassion, particularly in his efforts to prevent harm to his brother Joseph. While he participates in the plot against Joseph, Reuben ultimately intervenes to spare his life, advocating for his brother's safety. His sense of responsibility as the eldest son drives him to confront his brothers and acknowledge divine retribution for their actions.

Classical rabbinical literature further portrays Reuben as a figure of virtue, attributing the establishment of the first cities of refuge to his attempts to save Joseph from harm. His actions reflect a deep sense of duty and protectiveness toward his family, despite the complexities of their relationships.

Reuben's legacy extends beyond his mortal life, as classical sources attribute specific dates to his birth and death, alongside accounts of his burial in Israel. These narratives serve to immortalize Reuben's memory, emphasizing his enduring significance within the tapestry of Israelite history.

Territorial Inheritance:

In the biblical accounts, the Tribe of Reuben, alongside Gad and half of Manasseh, was granted land by Moses on the eastern side of the Jordan River and the Dead Sea. According to the Book of Joshua, Reuben's territory extended eastward from the Arnon River in the south to the northern reaches of the Dead Sea, encompassing the expansive plain of Madaba. However, the eastern border of Reuben's land was vaguely defined, dissolving into the desert expanse.

The delineation of borders between Reuben and the neighboring Tribe of Gad presents some inconsistencies within biblical texts. While certain passages assign Dibon and Aroer to Gad, others attribute these territories to Reuben. This discrepancy has led to interpretations suggesting that Reuben's territory may have been an enclave within the larger domain of Gad.

Scholars offer various explanations for these discrepancies. Yohanan Aharoni proposes that the descriptions in Numbers, placing Reubenites near Heshbon and surrounded by Gadites, reflect the actual settlement patterns during David's reign. Conversely, the descriptions in Joshua are seen as administrative districts established during Solomon's time, not accurately reflecting tribal boundaries.

By the 9th century BCE, historical records indicate that portions of Reuben and Gad's territories had fallen under the control of the Moabite kingdom. This geopolitical shift underscores the fluidity of territorial control and the dynamic interactions among ancient kingdoms in the region.

Throughout biblical texts, Reuben's territory is depicted as a land of abundance, conducive to the sustenance and prosperity of its inhabitants. From the fertile valleys to the grazing fields, Reuben's inheritance represented a sanctuary for its people, a testament to the fulfillment of divine promises.

Reuben's Role: From Conquests to Exile

During a pivotal period in ancient history, the Tribe of Reuben found itself entangled in significant events that shaped the narrative of Israelite existence. The ancient Song of Deborah vividly captures a moment when Reuben, though burdened with a heavy heart, chose not to engage in the battle against Sisera. Instead, they remained idle, tending to their flocks, as if oblivious to the tumultuous times.

Suddenly, Nahash, king of the Ammonites, emerged as a formidable aggressor, launching an attack on Jabesh-Gilead, a territory beyond his claimed domain. The inhabitants, besieged and desperate, sought terms of surrender, only to be met with a cruel ultimatum: death or the gouging out of their right eyes. In a desperate plea for help, messengers were dispatched throughout the land, and Saul, a humble herdsman at the time, answered the call. With a hastily raised army, Saul decisively defeated Nahash and his forces at Bezek, securing a victory for the oppressed.

The harsh tactics employed by Nahash were not isolated incidents but rather reflective of his customary practices, as elucidated by historical accounts and the discovery of ancient texts. The Dead Sea Scrolls shed light on Nahash's relentless campaign, highlighting the brutal oppression inflicted upon the descendants of Gad and Reuben. Despite the widespread suffering, a brave few managed to escape, seeking refuge in Jabesh-Gilead.

Throughout subsequent eras, the Tribe of Reuben continued to play a significant role in Israelite affairs. Chronicles chronicles their participation as valiant warriors in David's conquest of the City of David, demonstrating their unwavering loyalty and military prowess. Additionally, during King Saul's reign, Reuben engaged in victorious battles against the Hagarites, aided by Gad and the eastern half of Manasseh, as recounted in the annals of Chronicles.

However, the tide of fortune shifted for Reuben with the rise of Tiglath-Pileser III of Assyria, who orchestrated the deportation of Reubenites, Gadites, and half of Manasseh to distant lands. This forced exile marked a tumultuous chapter in Reuben's history, uprooting them from their ancestral homeland and scattering them across foreign territories.

The Moabite Mesha Stele provides further insight into the tribulations faced by Reuben, as the Moabites reclaimed territories once occupied by Israelite tribes. The absence of Reuben from the Stele's account suggests that by this time, the tribe had lost its distinct identity and territory, rendering it indistinguishable from neighboring forces.

In retrospect, the fate of Reuben serves as a poignant reminder of the fragility of tribal existence and the enduring struggles of ancient peoples. From conquests to exile, Reuben's journey encapsulates the triumphs and tribulations of a tribe caught in the ebb and flow of history's tide.

Conclusion: the Tribe of Reuben

In conclusion, the Tribe of Reuben stands as a testament to the multifaceted nature of biblical narrative and cultural identity. From its ancestral origins to its territorial inheritance, Reuben's story offers a window into the complexities of ancient Israelite society and the enduring legacy of its tribes. As we delve into the annals of history, may we glean wisdom from Reuben's journey and embrace the richness of our heritage and identity.

Chapter 4: The Tribe of Simeon

The Tribe of Simeon, listed among the twelve tribes of Israel in
the Hebrew Bible, holds a unique place in biblical history and
scholarship. While traditionally considered one of the ten lost
tribes, its territory within the boundaries of the Tribe of Judah
complicates its classification. Let's embark on a journey
through the biblical narrative to uncover the story of Simeon.

Origins:

The Tribe of Simeon, purportedly descended from Jacob's son
Simeon and Leah, occupies a significant yet enigmatic place
within the Hebrew Bible. However, interpretations regarding its
historical origins and narratives diverge among scholars,
shedding light on the complexities of biblical interpretation.

Arthur Peake's proposition challenges traditional
understandings by suggesting that the narratives concerning
Jacob's sons in Genesis might encode later tribal histories
(source). This viewpoint implies that the biblical accounts may
reflect broader tribal identities rather than individual
genealogies, adding layers of complexity to Simeon's story.

Regarding the allocation of land following the purported
conquest of Canaan, debates among scholars abound. While
conservative scholars like Kenneth Kitchen date the event to
around 1200 BCE, the prevailing consensus questions the
historicity of the conquest narrative as described in the Book of
Joshua. This scholarly discourse underscores the ongoing
reassessment of biblical chronology and events.

Martin Noth's theory regarding an amphictyonic association
among tribes, including Simeon, before the formation of the
Israelite confederacy, provides an intriguing lens through which
to interpret early Israelite history. However, dissenting voices
within academia challenge this hypothesis, signaling ongoing
debates and revisions in scholarly understanding.

The absence of explicit mentions of Simeon in ancient texts like the Song of Deborah raises further questions about the tribe's prominence and participation in early Israelite confederacies. Some scholars propose regional insignificance or possible non-alignment with the Israelite coalition as explanations for Simeon's absence from certain narratives, highlighting the complexities of tribal dynamics in ancient Israel.

In navigating the intricate tapestry of biblical narratives and scholarly interpretations, the story of the Tribe of Simeon emerges as a multifaceted and evolving aspect of Israelite history. As scholars continue to unravel its mysteries, we gain deeper insights into the complexities of ancient Israelite society and the construction of biblical narratives.

Territory:

The territorial allotment of the Tribe of Simeon within the Promised Land is outlined in the Book of Joshua. However, unlike many other tribes, Simeon's inheritance was not contiguous but rather consisted of scattered cities within the territory of Judah. This dispersion is attributed to various factors, including the size of the tribe and its historical actions. The cities within Judah's borders provided ample space for the tribe's descendants to dwell, albeit in a decentralized manner.

Situated in the southwest of Canaan, the territory of the Tribe of Simeon bordered the tribe of Judah to the east and south. However, the precise delineation of its boundaries remains ambiguous, with suggestions that Simeon may have functioned as an enclave within Judah's territory. Despite its proximity, Simeon held less significance within the Kingdom of Judah compared to other tribes.

Scholarly efforts to reconstruct Simeon's territory rely on biblical lists found in the Book of Joshua and 1 Chronicles. These lists delineate towns associated with Simeon, often overlapping with Judah's territory. Interpretations differ, with some scholars considering these lists as reflective of different historical periods, while others propose alternative perspectives on Simeon's settlement patterns.

Nadav Na'aman's analysis (Source) delineates two main schools of thought regarding Simeon's territorial boundaries. The "Alt school" interprets Joshua 15 as a later attempt to define Simeon's territory, while the "other school" views it as reflective of the historical situation during David's reign. Regardless of scholarly debate, evidence suggests that Simeonites maintained a distinct tribal identity while coexisting with Judahites, shaping the landscape of ancient Israel until the First Temple period.

Biblical Narrative:

According to biblical accounts, the Tribe of Simeon emerged as part of the Israelites' journey following the Exodus. However, scholarly interpretations vary regarding its origins and early history. From the Book of Genesis to the Babylonian captivity, the Bible offers glimpses into the tribe's existence, after which it fades from historical records. Extrabiblical Jewish sources provide supplementary information, enriching our understanding of Simeon's role within ancient Israel.

The Book of Joshua presents a puzzling scenario regarding the towns associated with the Tribe of Simeon, as they are also attributed to Judah in other sections. Modern scholars widely regard the Book of Joshua as a compilation of diverse source texts, suggesting that these discrepancies may stem from the merging of different documents from varying periods.

Evidently, the tribe experienced a significant decline in size over time, as indicated by the stark contrast in population between the two censuses recorded in the Book of Numbers. While biblical tradition places these censuses during the Exodus, scholars debate their authorship, with some attributing them to the Priestly Source, dated to the late 8th to 7th centuries BCE by Richard Elliot Freedman. Others situate this source in the post-exilic period or question its existence altogether.

The Books of Chronicles offer glimpses into the tribe's mobility and interactions. References suggest internal migrations, such as the movement of some members to Gedor in search of better pasture, as well as conflicts with neighboring peoples, notably during the reign of Hezekiah. These narratives reflect the dynamic nature of ancient Israelite society and the fluidity of tribal boundaries.

Following the Babylonian captivity, the remnants of Simeon became integrated into the broader Jewish identity within the Kingdom of Judah. Any distinctiveness that may have remained was overshadowed by a collective Jewish identity, emphasizing unity amidst adversity.

In a fascinating biblical echo, the Tribe of Simeon resurfaces in the Book of Revelation among the Twelve Tribes of Israel, symbolically sealed with 12,000 individuals. This depiction underscores the enduring presence and significance of Simeon within the eschatological framework of biblical prophecy.

As we piece together the fragmented narratives and scholarly interpretations, the story of the Tribe of Simeon emerges as a testament to the complexities of ancient Israelite history and the ongoing quest to unravel its mysteries.

Conclusion:

The Tribe of Simeon occupies a distinctive place in biblical history, characterized by a complex interplay of strengths and weaknesses. From its origins in the patriarchal era to its role in the conquest and settlement of the Promised Land, Simeon's legacy is one of resilience and determination amidst adversity.

Though dispersed among the territory of Judah, the descendants of Simeon remained an integral part of the Israelite nation, contributing to its cultural and religious tapestry.

Through their triumphs and trials, the Tribe of Simeon exemplifies the enduring saga of the chosen people and the intricate tapestry of biblical history.

Chapter 5: The Tribe of Levi

In the tapestry of biblical history, the Tribe of Levi stands as a pillar of sacred duty and divine service. Revered among the twelve tribes of Israel, their lineage carries a profound significance intertwined with the spiritual fabric of ancient Israelite society. As both a tribe and a priestly caste, the Levites played a pivotal role in shaping religious rituals, preserving traditions, and safeguarding the sanctity of worship. Let us embark on a journey through the annals of time to unravel the mysteries and majesty of the Tribe of Levi.

Origins and Lineage:

The roots of the Tribe of Levi trace back to the patriarch Levi, one of the twelve sons of Jacob (Israel). Born to Leah, Jacob's first wife, Levi emerged as a central figure in the narrative of Genesis, albeit not always for noble reasons. Nevertheless, it is through Levi's descendants that a sacred legacy would be forged, transcending his personal failings.

Levi, renowned in biblical narratives as a pivotal figure among the sons of Jacob, embodies the profound legacy of the Israelite Tribe of Levi. As recounted in the Book of Genesis, he emerges as the founder of this esteemed tribe and serves as the progenitor of illustrious descendants, including Aaron, Moses, and Miriam. Within the intricate tapestry of Israelite history, the Tribe of Levi assumes a distinct role, marked by sacred duties and revered lineage.

Delving into the origins of Levi's name unveils intriguing layers of interpretation. While the Torah suggests a connection to Leah's aspiration for union with Jacob, scholars speculate on alternative meanings. Some propose "priest" as a plausible interpretation, evoking the sacred role that would characterize the Levites in later narratives. Additionally, the Book of Jubilees provides a specific date for Levi's birth, further enriching the tapestry of his life.

The narrative of Levi unfolds with dramatic intensity in the Book of Genesis, notably in the aftermath of Dinah's violation in the city of Shechem. Alongside his brother Simeon, Levi orchestrates a vengeful retribution against the perpetrators, culminating in the city's devastation. However, Jacob's response encapsulates a complex blend of paternal rebuke and prophetic utterance, foretelling the Levites' scattered destiny as a consequence of their actions.

The genealogical accounts of Levi provide insight into the familial lineage that shaped his legacy. Fathering three sons – Gershon, Kohath, and Merari – Levi lays the groundwork for a lineage destined for significant roles within Israelite society. Notably, Kohath's descendants, including Amram and Jochebed, play instrumental roles in the narratives of Moses, Aaron, and Miriam, exemplifying the intertwining of familial ties and divine providence.

Beyond the canonical texts, apocryphal literature offers additional insights into Levi's familial relationships, including the mention of his wife, Milkah, in texts such as the Testaments of the Twelve Patriarchs and the Book of Jubilees. The Book of Jasher presents Adinah as Levi's wife, further enriching the mosaic of his familial connections.

Levitical Priesthood:

Central to the identity of the Tribe of Levi is their designation as the priestly class among the Israelites. According to the Book of Exodus, during the time of the Israelites' sojourn in Egypt, the Levites remained faithful to God during the period of enslavement and oppression. As a reward for their loyalty, they were chosen by God to serve as priests and intermediaries between the Israelites and the divine.

The Levitical priesthood was not merely an inherited title but a sacred responsibility passed down from generation to generation. Their duties encompassed various aspects of religious observance, including offering sacrifices, maintaining the Tabernacle or Temple, teaching the law, and conducting purification rituals. Their role was indispensable in facilitating communion between God and His chosen people.

Beyond their priestly duties, the Levites fulfilled diverse functions within Israelite society. They served as custodians of sacred artifacts, guardians of sacred spaces, and educators in matters of faith and law. Additionally, they played a vital role in the musical and liturgical aspects of worship, leading choirs and orchestras in praise of the Almighty.

Moreover, the Tribe of Levi was not allotted a territorial inheritance like the other tribes. Instead, they were dispersed throughout the land, residing in cities strategically positioned to provide spiritual guidance and support to the wider community. This dispersion underscored their role as spiritual shepherds, ensuring that the light of divine truth reached every corner of the land.

Legacy and Influence:

The legacy of the Tribe of Levi reverberates throughout biblical history and beyond. Their unwavering commitment to God's service, dedication to preserving sacred traditions, and tireless efforts to impart wisdom and guidance continue to inspire generations of believers.

Furthermore, the significance of the Levitical priesthood transcends the confines of ancient Israel. Its principles of devotion, holiness, and service find resonance in various religious traditions, underscoring the universal relevance of its teachings.

In conclusion, the Tribe of Levi stands as a testament to the enduring power of faith and service. Their story is one of redemption, resilience, and reverence – a narrative woven into the very fabric of biblical history. As we reflect on their legacy, may we be inspired to emulate their devotion and uphold the values they held dear, ensuring that their sacred heritage endures for generations to come.

Chapter 6: The Tribe of Judah

The tribe of Judah, one of the twelve tribes of Israel, stands as a pillar of significance in biblical narratives and historical accounts. Revered for its rich heritage, deep symbolism, and pivotal role in shaping the destiny of the Jewish people, the tribe of Judah holds a prominent place in both religious and secular discourse. In this exploration, we delve into the geographical, historical, and symbolic dimensions of this remarkable tribe.

Judah (son of Jacob):

Judah, according to the Book of Genesis, was the fourth son of Jacob and Leah, and he is known as the founder of the Tribe of Judah among the Israelites. His name, Yehuda in Hebrew, means "thanksgiving" or "praise," reflecting his mother Leah's sentiments upon his birth. He played a significant role in biblical narratives, particularly in the story of Joseph, where he suggested selling Joseph to Ishmaelite traders rather than killing him. Following his birth, Judah's next appearance is in Gen 37, when he and his brothers cast Joseph into a pit out of jealousy after Joseph approaches them, flaunting a coat of many colors, while they are working in the field.

Judah married a Canaanite woman named Aliyath and had three sons: Er, Onan, and Shelah. Er married Tamar but died, and his brother Onan also passed away for not fulfilling his duty to Tamar. When Judah did not allow Tamar to marry Shelah, she deceived him into fathering children with her. From this union came Perez and Zerah, with Perez being the ancestor of the messiah according to the Book of Ruth.

Later, Judah played a crucial role in securing Benjamin's release when Joseph, who had risen to power in Egypt, tested his brothers. Judah offered himself as surety for Benjamin's safety, ultimately revealing his compassion and leadership qualities. Jacob, their father, blessed Judah, predicting his future leadership and influence over his brothers.

In summary, Judah's story encompasses themes of family dynamics, loyalty, and divine providence, contributing to the foundational narratives of the Israelite people and the eventual emergence of the Kingdom of Judah.

Geographical Context:

The tribe of Judah resided in the southern region of ancient Israel, encompassing territories that included the city of Jerusalem. Its land stretched from the Dead Sea in the east to the Mediterranean coast in the west. The topography varied, ranging from fertile valleys to rugged mountains, providing a diverse landscape that influenced the tribe's livelihood and culture.

In its prime, the tribe of Judah stood as the foremost tribe within the Kingdom of Judah, dominating most of its territory. Apart from a small area in the northeast, occupied by Benjamin, and a southwestern enclave held by Simeon, the tribe of Judah encompassed much of the kingdom's lands. Key cities within its domain included Bethlehem and Hebron.

Geographically, the tribal lands of Judah were diverse and rich in resources:

1. The Negev, meaning "south," comprised the southern expanse, ideal for grazing and pastoral activities.
2. The Shephelah, or lowland, situated along the coast between the highlands and the Mediterranean Sea, was fertile ground for agriculture, particularly for growing grains.
3. The wilderness, adjacent to the Dead Sea and below sea level, presented a rugged and harsh environment, attracting wild animals and outlaws. This region, including subdivisions like the wilderness of En Gedi, Judah, and Maon, was scarcely inhabited.

4.   The hill country, lying between the Shephelah and the wilderness, featured rocky slopes but incredibly fertile soil. It was utilized for cultivation, yielding grains, olives, grapes, and other fruits, thereby contributing to the production of oil and wine.

In the Bible, Shicron marked one of the landmarks at the western extremity of Judah's northern boundary, possibly located near Ekron, underscoring the territorial delineations of the tribe.

Historical Significance:

Judah's history is intertwined with the broader narrative of Israelite history. According to biblical accounts, Judah was the fourth son of Jacob and Leah, born in the land of Canaan. The tribe gained prominence with the leadership of figures such as King David and King Solomon, who established Jerusalem as the capital of the united kingdom of Israel. Following the kingdom's division, Judah became the nucleus of the southern kingdom of Judah, maintaining its sovereignty for centuries until its eventual conquest by Babylon in 586 BCE.

The tribe of Judah holds a prominent position in biblical history, particularly in the Deuteronomistic narrative found in the books of Deuteronomy through II Kings. This history, widely believed to have been compiled during the reign of Josiah, a reformer in Judah during the 7th century BCE, highlights Judah's conquests and the significance of Jerusalem as the focal point for Yahweh worship.

In the Book of Joshua, although there is debate among scholars regarding the historical accuracy of the conquest accounts, Judah is portrayed as receiving a substantial portion of the southern region of Israel, including Jerusalem, following the division of land among the twelve tribes. Additionally, the Book of Judges depicts Judah as the first tribe to occupy its allotted territory, engaging in alliances with other tribes, notably Simeon.

The lineage of Judah gains further importance in the Book of Samuel, where God rejects Saul's descendants from ruling and instead chooses David from the tribe of Judah as the eternal monarch. Despite initial divisions among the tribes, David's kingship ultimately unites them under a single kingdom, reaching its zenith during Solomon's reign.

However, tensions arise after Solomon's death, leading to the division of the kingdom into the Northern and Southern Kingdoms. The tribes of Judah and Benjamin remain loyal to the House of David, forming the Kingdom of Judah, while the other ten tribes establish the Northern Kingdom. Eventually, Judah fell to Babylonian conquest in 586 BCE, leading to the exile of its inhabitants.

Upon their return from Babylon, tribal affiliations diminish, but religious roles are retained. Jerusalem becomes the focal point of worship for all returning exiles, emphasizing the unity of the Jewish people in their religious practices despite the dissolution of tribal distinctions.

Despite the challenges of exile and dispersion, the tribe of Judah persisted through the ages, preserving its identity and contributing to the cultural tapestry of Judaism. The return from Babylonian exile marked a significant chapter in Judah's history, symbolizing resilience and renewal as the people rebuilt their temple and reestablished their community in the land of their forefathers.

Symbolism and Cultural Legacy:

The tribe of Judah is laden with symbolic significance, emblematic of strength, leadership, and spiritual devotion. The Lion of Judah, a powerful symbol derived from biblical prophecy, represents courage, sovereignty, and the messianic lineage traced through the Davidic monarchy. This symbol has resonated deeply within Jewish tradition and beyond, becoming an enduring emblem of resilience and hope.

Moreover, Judah holds a central place in religious rites and rituals, with its name invoked in prayers and blessings. The Torah describes Judah as the scepter-bearing tribe, suggesting its preeminence among the twelve tribes. Additionally, the tribe's association with the Davidic dynasty and the promised Messiah imbues it with messianic expectations, shaping eschatological beliefs and theological discourse.

Fate & Relevance Today:

As an integral part of the Kingdom of Judah, the tribe of Judah endured the Assyrian conquest of Israel and subsequently experienced the Babylonian exile. Following the end of the captivity, tribal distinctions faded in favor of a unified identity, ultimately leading to the emergence of the term "Jews," derived from the name of the dominant tribe, Judah.

After the fall of Jerusalem, Babylonia, situated in modern-day Iraq, became the epicenter of Jewish life for a millennium. The initial Jewish communities in Babylonia were established with the exile of the tribe of Judah to Babylon in 597 BCE, a trend that continued after the destruction of the Temple in Jerusalem in 586 BCE. Subsequent waves of Jewish migration to Babylon occurred, notably after the Bar Kokhba revolt in CE 135 and in the following centuries.

The imagery of the "Lion of the Tribe of Judah" achieving triumph is depicted in the Book of Revelation within the New Testament, symbolizing victory and divine authority.

Ethiopia's historical traditions, documented in the 13th-century work "Kebre Negest," claim descent from a group of Israelites who accompanied the Queen of Sheba back from her visit to King Solomon in Jerusalem. According to Ethiopian Christian and Jewish traditions, many of these immigrants belonged to the tribes of Dan and Judah. This heritage is reflected in the Ge'ez motto "Mo'a 'Anbessa Ze'imnegede Yihuda" ("The Lion of the Tribe of Judah has conquered"), one of several names attributed to Jesus of Nazareth.

While the tribe of Judah's ancient territories may have transformed over millennia, its legacy endures in the hearts and minds of millions worldwide. From the sacred precincts of Jerusalem to the dispersed communities across the globe, Judah's influence permeates Jewish identity and collective memory.

Furthermore, the tribe of Judah serves as a reminder of the enduring power of faith, community, and heritage in navigating the complexities of history and identity. Its story resonates with themes of perseverance, redemption, and divine providence, offering timeless lessons for contemporary generations seeking meaning and connection in an ever-changing world.

In conclusion, the tribe of Judah stands as a beacon of spiritual and cultural significance, embodying the storied legacy of the Jewish people. From its ancestral homelands to the farthest reaches of the diaspora, Judah's journey echoes through the corridors of history, inspiring awe and reverence for generations to come.

Chapter 7: The Tribe of Issachar

In the tapestry of ancient Israelite history, the Tribe of Issachar remains a fascinating yet often overlooked thread. Their story, woven intricately into the narrative of the Old Testament, offers profound insights into the socio-political landscape of ancient Israel. Let's embark on a journey to explore the legacy of the Tribe of Issachar, uncovering their significance and contributions to the broader narrative of the Israelites.

Origins and Genealogy:

Issachar, as depicted in the Book of Genesis, emerges as a pivotal figure in the ancestral lineage of the Israelite Tribe of Issachar. The etymology of his name, laden with symbolic significance, invites scholarly inquiry and interpretation, reflecting the complexities inherent in biblical narratives. Two distinct etymologies, attributed to different textual sources, offer insights into the perceived significance of Issachar's birth within the context of Jacob's familial dynamics.

The first etymology, derived from "ish sakar," meaning "man of hire," alludes to the transactional nature of Jacob and Leah's relationship, symbolized by the exchange of mandrakes for Jacob's conjugal favors. This interpretation underscores the pragmatic nature of Issachar's origins, portraying him as a product of contractual arrangements within the household. Alternatively, the interpretation of "yesh sakar," meaning "there is a reward," emphasizes the divine blessing bestowed upon Leah for her sacrifice in giving her handmaid, Zilpah, to Jacob. This perspective elevates Issachar's birth as a testament to divine providence, reinforcing the notion of spiritual recompense within the biblical narrative.

Historical theories surrounding Issachar's origins further enrich our understanding of his significance within the Israelite confederation. While biblical accounts position Issachar as one of the original tribes of Israel, textual discrepancies and

47

scholarly analysis suggest alternative hypotheses. Some scholars propose a connection between the tribe of Issachar and the Shekelesh group of Sea Peoples, positing a non-Israelite origin for Issachar. This theory, supported by linguistic and historical evidence, underscores the fluidity of ethnic and cultural identities in the ancient Near East, challenging conventional interpretations of Israelite tribal affiliations.

Rabbinical interpretations offer additional layers of insight into Issachar's character and legacy. Classical rabbinical literature portrays Issachar as a pragmatic and scholarly figure, exemplifying dedication to Torah study and spiritual pursuits. His marriage to Aridah, the daughter of Jobab, symbolizes alliances forged through kinship and lineage, further embedding Issachar within the socio-political landscape of his time. The Talmudic interpretation of Issachar as a "strong ass lying down between two burdens" highlights the tribe's renowned religious scholarship, affirming their role as custodians of spiritual knowledge and wisdom.

In conclusion, the figure of Issachar transcends mere genealogical lineage, embodying themes of divine providence, cultural identity, and scholarly pursuit within the tapestry of biblical narrative. As we delve deeper into his story, we uncover layers of complexity and nuance that illuminate the enduring significance of Issachar within the annals of Israelite history and collective memory.

Territorial Inheritance:

During the conquest of Canaan under the leadership of Joshua, the land allotted to the Tribe of Issachar lay in the northern part of the land, nestled between the territories of Zebulun and Naphtali. Their inheritance included fertile plains and valleys, conducive to agriculture and trade, which played a crucial role in their economic prosperity and sustenance.

In the biblical narrative recounted in the Book of Joshua, the land apportioned to Issachar stretched from the Jordan River to Mount Carmel, encompassing the fertile Esdraelon plain. Situated strategically between East Manasseh, West Manasseh, Zebulun, and Naphtali, this territory served as a vital nexus for trade and cultural exchange, shaping the economic and geopolitical landscape of ancient Israel.

Role and Contributions:

The Tribe of Issachar played a significant role in the early history of Israel. They were renowned for their wisdom, discernment, and understanding of the times, as chronicled in the Song of Deborah found in the book of Judges. Deborah, a prophetess and judge in Israel, praised Issachar for their willingness to join the fight against oppression under the leadership of Barak, demonstrating their commitment to the collective welfare of the nation.

Furthermore, Issachar's strategic location at the crossroads of trade routes facilitated commerce and cultural exchange, enriching both their community and the wider Israelite society. Their shrewdness in navigating political alliances and economic ventures contributed to the stability and prosperity of the Israelite Confederation during various periods of its history.

The Tribe of Issachar distinguished itself not only through its territorial inheritance but also through its intellectual prowess and spiritual insight. Described in 1 Chronicles 12:32 as men "who had understanding of the times, to know what Israel ought to do," Issachar's scholars and leaders were renowned for their discernment and wisdom. Rabbinic literature further illuminates their legacy, portraying Issachar as a tribe dominated by scholars deeply engaged in the study of Torah. Their influence extended beyond scholarly pursuits, as they played a pivotal role in proselytism and the dissemination of Jewish teachings.

Rooted in their devotion to Torah study and spiritual practice, the Tribe of Issachar upheld a sacred legacy passed down from their forefathers. Rabbinic interpretations of Jacob's blessing (Genesis 49:14-15) highlight Issachar's dedication to Torah learning, positioning them as custodians of divine wisdom within the community. Despite their scholarly pursuits, Issachar remained actively engaged in the affairs of their people, providing leadership and counsel during times of decision-making and national significance.

In conclusion, the Tribe of Issachar occupies a significant place in the tapestry of Israelite history. Their wisdom, discernment, and strategic prowess, coupled with their spiritual heritage, distinguish them as a tribe of great importance. As we delve into the annals of biblical history, let us not overlook the enduring legacy of Issachar and the invaluable lessons they impart to us today. May their story inspire us to seek wisdom, discern the times, and remain steadfast in our commitment to God and His purposes.

Chapter 8: The Tribe of Zebulun

In the rich tapestry of biblical history, certain tribes often capture more attention than others. However, amidst the tales of Judah, Ephraim, and Benjamin, lies a tribe whose significance is often overlooked—the Tribe of Zebulun. In this chapter, we embark on a journey to uncover the hidden treasures and remarkable contributions of the Tribe of Zebulun to the story of Israel.

Origins and Genealogy:

Zebulun, the sixth son of Jacob and Leah, stands as the patriarch of the Israelite tribe bearing his name. Rooted in ancient biblical narratives, the tribe of Zebulun holds a unique place within the fabric of Israelite history and culture.

The significance of Zebulun extends beyond mere genealogy, with scholars debating the metaphorical underpinnings of its name. Some suggest it reflects the tribe's interconnectedness within the Israelite confederation, a notion reinforced by its matriarchal lineage traced back to Leah.

The etymology of Zebulun's name offers multiple interpretations, hinting at its complex linguistic origins. Whether derived from words connoting "gift," "honor," or "sacrifice," each proposed meaning sheds light on the tribe's character and aspirations.

Notably, the tomb of Zebulun resides in Sidon, Lebanon, serving as a sacred site of pilgrimage for Jews, symbolizing the enduring spiritual ties to their ancestral heritage.

Scripture credits Zebulun with three sons, each representing a distinct clan within the tribe's lineage. These descendants inherited the legacy of their forefather, embodying the spirit of courage and sacrifice exemplified in the Song of Deborah.

51

Indeed, Zebulun's valor on the battlefield alongside Naphtali echoes through the ages, immortalized in the stirring verses of ancient poetry. Their willingness to risk life and limb reflects a deep-seated commitment to the collective defense and honor of their people.

Territory and Inheritance:

The Tribe of Zebulun played a crucial role in the early history of Israel, as chronicled in the Torah. During the census in the Desert of Sinai, conducted in the second year of the Exodus, Zebulun contributed a formidable force of 57,400 men ready for war, commanded by Eliab the son of Helon. This army, positioned alongside Judah and Issachar, formed the vanguard during the journey through the wilderness. Additionally, when Moses dispatched spies to survey Canaan, Gaddiel represented Zebulun among them.

Following the incident at Shittim in the land of Moab, where a second census was taken after the death of 24,000 men, Zebulun's fighting force had increased to 60,500. Elizaphan the son of Parnach was appointed to represent the tribe during the division of the Promised Land.

Throughout the era of Joshua's leadership, Zebulun received no special mention until the time of the Song of Deborah. Here, the tribe is lauded for their bravery in battle, particularly in the region of Merom, and praised for providing officers instrumental in military operations. Zebulun's involvement in significant conflicts, such as Barak's campaign against Sisera and participation in Gideon's battle against Midian, highlights their martial prowess and dedication to the nation.

During the reign of David, Zebulun demonstrated unwavering loyalty by contributing 50,000 fully armed men to support his ascension to the throne. Furthermore, when Hezekiah initiated religious reforms, representatives from Zebulun journeyed to Jerusalem to participate in the Passover celebrations and help cleanse the land of idolatry.

In terms of territory, Zebulun's allotment was significant, starting with Sarid (possibly Tel Shadud), approximately five miles southwest of Nazareth. Although the exact boundaries are not entirely clear, Josephus suggests their territory extended near Carmel and the Sea of Galilee. This region, nestled between Asher and Issachar, encompassed portions of the Jezreel Valley and served as a crucial thoroughfare from the sea to the lake.

Within this territory, the village of Bethlehem of Galilee is identified with certainty, and it is believed to be where Jesus spent his formative years, fulfilling numerous prophecies and teachings recorded in the Gospels, particularly in the Synoptics, during his Galilean ministry. Thus, the land of Zebulun holds not only historical significance but also spiritual importance in the narrative of Christianity.

Characteristics and Attributes:

In the ancient Song of Deborah, Zebulun is depicted as dispatching warriors skilled in the handling of the sopher shebet. This phrase has traditionally been interpreted as referring to those who wielded the "rod of the scribe," an instrument used for writing on various mediums such as clay tablets or papyrus. These individuals were likely associates or assistants of lawgivers, contributing to legal and administrative duties.

In Jewish tradition, the Tribe of Zebulun was believed to have a symbiotic relationship with its neighboring tribe, Issachar. Issachar, renowned for its scholars and dedication to Torah study, received financial support from Zebulun in exchange for a share of the spiritual rewards derived from such learning. This partnership became symbolic, with "Issachar and Zebulun" representing anyone engaged in a similar relationship of support and study.

While some interpretations suggest Zebulun sent those adept at military leadership, recent Christian scholarship has leaned towards translating the Song of Deborah differently, portraying Zebulun as sending officers to battle rather than scribe-like figures.

This partnership between Issachar and Zebulun also touches upon ideological debates within Jewish thought. Some argue that spiritual rewards in the afterlife can be exchanged for material support in the present, while others maintain that such rewards cannot be bartered.

The collaboration between Zebulun and Naphtali is also a recurring theme in biblical narratives. The Book of Judges recounts how Deborah, a prophetess and judge, summoned Barak from the tribe of Naphtali and instructed him to gather men from his tribe and from Zebulun to confront the Canaanite forces under Sisera's command (Judges 4:6). This alliance led to a decisive victory for Israel, demonstrating the strength that unity among the tribes could yield.

Conclusion:

In conclusion, while the Tribe of Zebulun may not occupy center stage in biblical accounts, its significance in Israel's history should not be underestimated. Through their maritime prowess, collaboration with neighboring tribes, and participation in the spiritual life of the nation, the Zebulunites contributed to the flourishing of Israelite society. As we delve deeper into the stories of these unsung heroes, we uncover valuable lessons about unity, perseverance, and the diverse roles within the tapestry of God's chosen people. Let us remember the Tribe of Zebulun with honor and appreciation for their part in the grand narrative of biblical history.

Chapter 9: The Tribe of Dan

In the annals of ancient Israelite history, the Tribe of Dan stands as a fascinating enigma, shrouded in both mystery and significance. From its origins as one of the twelve tribes of Israel to its eventual dispersion and various historical connections, the story of Dan is a rich tapestry woven into the fabric of Israel's past. Join us as we embark on a journey through time to explore the intriguing history of the Tribe of Dan.

Origins:

According to the biblical account found in the Book of Genesis, Dan was one of the twelve sons of Jacob. As such, Dan was a full-fledged tribe within the confederation of Israelite tribes, each tracing their lineage back to one of Jacob's sons.

Dan, as depicted in the Book of Genesis, emerges as a significant figure within the lineage of the Israelites. Born to Jacob and Bilhah, Rachel's handmaid, Dan's name carries a profound meaning, stemming from Rachel's belief that his birth was a divine judgment, symbolized by the name's translation, "he has judged me."

Throughout biblical narratives, Dan's character is portrayed with complexity. References in the Book of Judges highlight Dan's involvement in certain religious practices and the deviation of some of its members, such as Samson, from prescribed norms. These instances led classical rabbinical writers to view Dan as a figure outside the norm, often associated with moral ambiguity and deviation from righteousness.

Apocryphal texts further explore Dan's persona, depicting him as harboring animosity towards his brother Joseph and playing a role in deceiving their father Jacob. Symbolically, Dan is likened to a serpent in the Blessing of Jacob, a metaphor that underscores the complexities of his character and his potential for both good and evil.

Early Christian theologians, such as Irenaeus and Hippolytus, even speculated that the Antichrist would emerge from Dan's lineage, further complicating the perception of this biblical figure. John the Apostle's omission of the Tribe of Dan from his listing of the twelve tribes of Israel, instead opting to include Joseph twice, adds another layer of mystery to Dan's story, sparking interpretations and discussions among scholars and theologians throughout history.

In conclusion, the portrayal of Dan as an individual within the biblical tradition is filled with symbolism, complexity, and theological speculation. His story invites exploration into the nuances of human nature, morality, and the enduring themes of judgment and redemption present throughout biblical narratives.

Migration and Settlement:

One of the most intriguing aspects of Dan's history is its migration patterns and settlement. While many of the tribes were allocated specific territories within the Promised Land, the Tribe of Dan encountered challenges in securing its inheritance. The biblical narrative in Judges 18 recounts how the Danites, dissatisfied with their allotted territory, sent scouts to search for a more suitable land to inhabit. This eventually led them to conquer the city of Laish in the far north of Israel, which they renamed Dan, establishing a new settlement in the process.

In the census recorded in the Book of Numbers, the Tribe of Dan holds a significant position as the second largest Israelite tribe, following Judah. Scholars debate the dating of this census, with some attributing it to the Priestly Source around the 7th century BC, potentially reflecting the biases of its authors. Additionally, in the Blessing of Moses, which likely predates the Deuteronomist, Dan is prophesied to "leap from

Bashan," a puzzling assertion given that the tribe did not inhabit the Bashan plain east of the Jordan River.

Following the completion of the Israelite conquest of Canaan, Joshua distributed the land among the twelve tribes. Dan, however, received its inheritance last. Initially allocated a small enclave in the central coastal region of Canaan, the tribe's territory was bordered by Judah, Benjamin, Ephraim, and the Philistines. Despite attempts to settle in this area, pressure from the Philistines forced a portion of the tribe to migrate northward.

Led by the legendary judge Samson, the Danites settled in the north and conquered Laish, renaming it Dan. This relocation positioned them northeast of Naphtali, defining the northern extent of Israelite territory.

During the era of the united monarchy under Saul, the Tribe of Dan supported the centralization of power to counter Philistine threats. Following the deaths of Saul and his son Ish-bosheth, Dan, along with other northern tribes, pledged allegiance to David, leading to the formation of a reunited Kingdom of Israel.

However, tensions resurfaced upon the accession of Rehoboam, leading to the split of the kingdom into the Northern and Southern Kingdoms. The Tribe of Dan became part of the Northern Kingdom of Israel.

Ultimately, the Assyrian conquest resulted in the exile of the Tribe of Dan, leading to the loss of their historical records and further complicating the understanding of their fate.

Religious and Cultural Influence:

In addition to its territorial conquests, the Tribe of Dan also left its mark on Israelite religious and cultural practices. Dan was home to one of the most prominent sanctuaries in ancient Israel, the city of Dan, where Jeroboam I established a golden calf idol during the period of the divided monarchy. This act of religious innovation ultimately led to the schism between the northern kingdom of Israel and the southern kingdom of Judah, with Dan playing a pivotal role in the political and religious landscape of the region.

Modern artists use the "scales of justice" to represent the Tribe of Dan due to Genesis 49:16 referencing Dan "shall achieve justice for his kindred". More traditional artists use a snake to represent Dan, based upon Genesis 49:17, "Let Dan be a serpent by the roadside, a horned viper by the path, That bites the horse's heel, so that the rider tumbles backward."

Dispersal and Legacy:

Despite its early prominence, the Tribe of Dan eventually faced challenges that would lead to its decline. The biblical account in Judges depicts Dan as a tribe prone to idolatry and spiritual waywardness, which may have contributed to its diminished status over time. Additionally, historical records suggest that the Tribe of Dan was one of the first to be exiled following the Assyrian conquest of the northern kingdom of Israel, scattering its members across the ancient Near East.

The history of the Tribe of Dan offers a fascinating glimpse into the complexities of ancient Israelite society. From its origins as one of the twelve tribes of Israel to its migration, settlement, and eventual dispersal, Dan's story is one of resilience, innovation, and spiritual struggle. By exploring the rich tapestry of Dan's history, we gain valuable insights into the cultural, religious, and political dynamics of the ancient Near East, illuminating the enduring legacy of one of Israel's most enigmatic tribes.

Chapter 10: The Tribe of Naphtali

In the intricate mosaic of biblical narratives, certain tribes often shine brightly, while others remain in the shadows. Among the lesser-known yet significant tribes of Israel is Naphtali. In this exploration, we delve into the rich history and profound contributions of the Tribe of Naphtali, shedding light on its role and territory within the Israelite confederation.

Origins and Genealogy:

According to the Book of Genesis, Naphtali, the sixth son of Jacob, was born of Bilhah, Rachel's handmaid. The name "Naphtali" itself conveys a sense of struggle, reflecting the complex dynamics between Rachel and Leah, Jacob's wives, as they vied for his affection and favor.

Biblical commentators offer interpretations suggesting that Naphtali's birth may symbolize Rachel's longing for a child amid her infertility. Through Bilhah, Rachel sought to fulfill her maternal desires, resulting in the birth of Naphtali, who would go on to become the patriarch of a distinct Israelite tribe.

In the Blessing of Jacob, Naphtali is likened to a swift hind, suggesting agility and prowess. While some traditional interpretations view this as a personal trait of Naphtali himself, others see it as emblematic of the entire tribe's character, emphasizing their agility and adaptability in various circumstances.

Naphtali's family is briefly mentioned in Genesis 46:24, where he is recorded to have four sons: Jahzeel, Guni, Jezer, and Shillem. The details of his wife or wives are not provided in the biblical text. Together with his family, Naphtali journeyed to Egypt, where they settled alongside the rest of their clan, awaiting the moment of Exodus.

According to the apocryphal Testament of the Twelve Patriarchs, Naphtali lived to the age of 137 before passing away and being laid to rest in Egypt. Though his life is relatively sparsely documented in scripture, his descendants would play significant roles in the unfolding narrative of Israel's history, embodying the enduring legacy of their patriarch amid the struggles and triumphs of their journey.

Biblical Narrative & Territory:

The biblical narrative of the Tribe of Naphtali is woven with threads of conquest, settlement, and geopolitical upheaval, tracing their journey from the allocation of land under Joshua to their eventual dispersal as one of the Ten Lost Tribes of Israel.

Following the completion of the conquest of Canaan, Joshua distributed the land among the twelve tribes, with Naphtali settling on the eastern side of the Galilee, encompassing areas now known as the Lower and Upper Galilee. Bordered by Asher, Dan, Zebulun, and the Jordan River, Naphtali's territory boasted the significant city of Hazor and the fertile plains of Gennesaret, often likened to an earthly paradise by historians.

In the era of the Judges, Naphtali, like the other tribes, operated within a loose confederation without central governance. However, facing external threats such as Philistine incursions, the Israelite tribes united to establish a centralized monarchy, with Saul as their first king. Naphtali remained loyal to Saul's lineage until the ascension of David, who unified the kingdom.

Yet, political instability soon followed with the division of the kingdom after the reign of Rehoboam. Naphtali found itself within the Northern Kingdom, which later faced invasion and deportation by the Assyrians in 732 BCE. Tiglath-Pileser III's conquest led to the annexation of Aram and significant portions of Israel, including the land of Naphtali. The population endured deportation to Assyria, marking the beginning of their status as one of the Ten Lost Tribes.

Despite their dispersion, the legacy of Naphtali endures in biblical history, a testament to their resilience amidst the tumultuous currents of ancient geopolitics. The narrative of Naphtali serves as a poignant reminder of the ebb and flow of power, the fragility of kingdoms, and the enduring spirit of a people whose fate remains shrouded in mystery.

Role in Israelite History:

The Tribe of Naphtali emerges from biblical narratives as a testament to militarism and swiftness, embodying characteristics of courage and agility that left an indelible mark on Israelite history.

Though Naphtali may not feature prominently in every biblical account, its contributions to the nation of Israel are significant. In the Book of Judges, Naphtali is depicted as one of the tribes that responded to the call of Deborah and Barak to confront the oppressive forces of Sisera. Together with Zebulun, Naphtali played a pivotal role in securing victory for Israel, demonstrating bravery and solidarity in the face of adversity.

In the ancient Song of Deborah, Naphtali stands alongside Zebulun, earning commendation for their valorous efforts in the battle against Sisera. This depiction underscores their willingness to risk their lives for the cause of their people, a testament to their martial spirit and commitment to the defense of Israel. Furthermore, the tribe's association with Barak, the leader of the anti-Sisera forces, adds another layer of martial prowess to their character, highlighting their role in pivotal moments of conflict.

The Gideon narrative further showcases Naphtali's martial prowess, as they join forces with other tribes in an attack against Midianite invaders. Though textual scholars debate the historical accuracy of this account, the portrayal of Naphtali's involvement in battle underscores their reputation as fierce warriors.

In the Blessing of Jacob, Naphtali is likened to a hind let loose, symbolizing their swiftness and agility in both physical and metaphorical realms. Their ability to deliver "goodly words" further accentuates their reputation for eloquence and prowess in communication.

Geographically, Naphtali's territory in Canaan was situated in the extreme north, bordered by prominent landmarks such as the Litani River to the north and the River Jordan to the east. The symbol of the tribe—a gazelle—aptly reflects their reputation for speed and agility, both in the physical and metaphorical sense.

Overall, the Tribe of Naphtali emerged as a formidable force in Israelite history, characterized by their valor in battle, swiftness of action, and eloquence in communication. Their contributions to the defense and prosperity of Israel leave an enduring legacy, inspiring future generations with their courage and resilience.

In conclusion, the Tribe of Naphtali may be one of the lesser-known tribes of Israel, but its impact on the nation's history and spiritual legacy is undeniable. From its ancestral territory in the Galilee to its valiant deeds on the battlefield, Naphtali played a vital role in the story of God's people. As we uncover the layers of its history and heritage, we gain valuable insights into the diversity and richness of Israelite culture and the enduring significance of its tribal identity.

Chapter 11: The Tribe of Gad

The Tribe of Gad, one of the twelve tribes of Israel, traces its lineage back to Gad, the seventh son of Jacob and the first son born to Zilpah, Leah's maidservant. The name Gad is thought to be derived from the Hebrew word for "luck" or "fortunate," reflecting the hope and promise associated with this tribe.

Biblical History and Origin:

In the biblical account found in Genesis, Gad's birth is marked by his mother Leah's gratitude, and his destiny intertwines with the broader narrative of the patriarchs. As the Israelites journeyed through the wilderness and settled in Canaan, the Tribe of Gad played a pivotal role in the unfolding drama of Israel's history.

In the epochs following the Exodus, the Tribe of Gad became an integral part of the loose confederation of Israelite tribes. The era, marked by the leadership of ad hoc figures known as Judges, saw the Gadites navigating challenges and alliances. One such event featured Nahash, the Ammonite king, laying siege to Jabesh-Gilead, demanding a choice between death and the gouging out of the right eye. The Gadites, led by Saul, responded with valor, defeating Nahash at Bezek and solidifying their place in the historical tapestry.

According to the Torah, the Tribe of Gad traces its ancestry to Gad, the seventh son of Jacob, from whom it derives its name. However, certain Biblical scholars interpret this lineage as a postdiction, suggesting that it serves as an eponymous metaphor explaining the tribal interconnectedness within the Israelite confederation. In the biblical narrative, Gad and Asher are depicted as descendants of Zilpah, a handmaid of Jacob, implying a potential non-Israelite origin due to their lineage through handmaids rather than full wives.

Similar to Asher, the geographic details associated with Gad exhibit diversity and discrepancies. Cities are at times attributed to Gad and at other times to different tribes, accompanied by inconsistent boundaries. The term "Gilead" itself fluctuates in its inclusion of Gad within its borders. The Moabite Stone further suggests a distinction between the kingdom of Israel and the tribe of Gad, implying an ancient presence predating Israel's settlement east of the Jordan.

These details hint at Gad's possible origin as a northward-migrating nomadic tribe during a period when other tribes had already settled in Canaan. In the biblical account, Gad's choice to settle east of the Jordan is explained by the tribe's immediate attraction to the land before crossing the Jordan under Joshua and participating in the conquest of Canaan. Classical rabbinical literature criticizes Gad for this decision, attributing it to a desire for immediate satisfaction akin to the rich being denied sleep with a full stomach.

Despite this criticism, when Gad crossed the river to assist their brethren in the conquest, they earned commendation. Moses was buried in the territory of Gad, and some traditions even identify Elijah as a descendant of Gad. Additionally, the tribes of Gad and Reuben were among the first to go into exile, marking a significant chapter in their history.

The Territory of Gad:

The land allocated to the Tribe of Gad was situated to the east of the Jordan River, encompassing fertile plains ideal for livestock and agriculture. This region, known for its abundance and strategic location, became the ancestral home of the Gadites. Despite being on the eastern side of the Jordan, the Tribe of Gad committed to supporting their fellow Israelites in the conquest and settlement of the promised land west of the Jordan.

After the successful completion of the Israelite tribes' conquest of Canaan around 1200 BCE, Joshua undertook the task of distributing the conquered land among the twelve tribes. However, a distinctive allocation was made for the Tribes of Gad, Reuben, and half of Manasseh. Moses had previously designated land for them on the eastern side of the Jordan River and the Dead Sea, as documented in Joshua 13:24–28. The Tribe of Gad specifically received a central region, situated east of Ephraim and west of Manasseh, although the precise location remains somewhat ambiguous.

The delineated border extended from Jazer, encompassing all the cities of Gilead and half the land of the children of Ammon, reaching Aroer before Rabbah. The boundary further included Heshbon, Ramath-Mizpah, Betonim, Mahanaim, Lidbir's border in the valley, Beth-haram, Beth-umrah, Succoth, and Zaphon. This expansive territory encapsulated the remnants of the kingdom of Sihon, the king of Heshbon, with the Jordan River serving as its western boundary, extending to the farthest point of the Sea of Chinnereth beyond the Jordan in the east.

Cities such as Ramoth, Jaezer, Aroer, and Dibon are noted in Numbers 32:34 as having, at some point, been part of the Tribe of Gad's territory. However, it's worth noting that the allocation of specific cities appears to vary, as Joshua 13:15–16 designates some of these locations as belonging to the Tribe of Reuben.

Despite the allotted land's strategic importance, security remained a constant concern. To the south, the Tribe of Gad faced exposure to the Moabites, while the northern and eastern fronts were vulnerable to the threats posed by Aram-Damascus and, later, the Assyrians. This susceptibility to invasion and attacks underscored the challenges faced by the tribes residing east of the Jordan River.

Fate of Tribe of Gad:

The fate of the Tribe of Gad takes center stage during the conquest of Canaan under the leadership of Joshua. As the other tribes secured their territories, the Gadites, along with the tribes of Reuben and half of the tribe of Manasseh, requested permission to settle on the east side of the Jordan, where their livestock could thrive. This request was granted, but not without the commitment of the Gadites to join their brethren in the west in the military campaigns to secure the land.

The Gadites fulfilled their promise, fighting alongside their fellow Israelites to establish a foothold in the promised land. Their dedication in battle exemplified the unity among the tribes of Israel. The Tribe of Gad's commitment to both their territorial inheritance and their covenantal obligations showcases the complex interplay between destiny and duty.

Conclusion:

The Tribe of Gad, with its roots in the ancient soil of Israel, contributes a vital chapter to the biblical narrative. From its origins to its role in the conquest of Canaan, Gad's story is one of perseverance, commitment, and the interdependence of a people united by a shared heritage. Exploring the fate of the Tribe of Gad opens a window into the larger tapestry of Israel's journey, offering valuable insights into the complexities of biblical history and the enduring legacy of this unique tribe.

Chapter 12: The Tribe of Asher

In the rich tapestry of ancient Israelite history, the Tribe of Asher emerges as a distinctive and intriguing entity. Located in the northern part of the Promised Land, the territory of Asher played a vital role in the biblical narrative, contributing to the cultural and historical mosaic of the Israelites.

Asher:

Asher, a significant figure in the Book of Genesis, occupies a unique place as the last of Jacob's sons with Zilpah, Jacob's eighth son, and the progenitor of the Israelite Tribe of Asher. The name "Asher" is associated with the Hebrew term "osher," meaning "happy" or "blessing." Leah, at Asher's birth, exclaims joyfully, "Happy am I! for the daughters will call me happy: so she called his name Asher" (Genesis 30:13). The etymology of the name reflects a sense of joy and good fortune, offering a glimpse into the aspirations and sentiments surrounding his birth.

The meaning of Asher's name has sparked discussions among textual scholars, with some attributing variations like "beoshri" and "ishsheruni" to different sources, possibly the Yahwist and the Elohist. There are intriguing theories regarding the deity associated with Asher's name, with suggestions ranging from Asherah to Ashur, the chief Assyrian deity, indicating a potential link with the tribe's religious practices.

In the biblical narrative, Asher, along with his four sons and daughter, settles in Canaan. Jacob, on his deathbed, bestows a blessing upon Asher, foreseeing prosperity and the enjoyment of royal delicacies (Genesis 49:20). Moses, in the book of Deuteronomy, further extends a blessing to Asher, emphasizing his esteemed position among his brothers and the abundance symbolized by olive oil (Deuteronomy 33:24).

Asher's familial lineage is carefully detailed, depicting him as the eighth son of Jacob and the younger brother of Gad. The complexity of Zilpah's status, initially a handmaid and later recognized as an actual wife of Jacob, raises questions about Asher's Israelite origin, with some scholars suggesting that the tribe may have consisted of clans affiliated with the Israelite tribal confederation but not fully integrated into the political structure.

Asher's life unfolds with the Torah mentioning his four sons—Jimnah, Ishuah, Isui, and Beriah—and a daughter, Serah. This daughter is notably the only granddaughter of Jacob explicitly named in the Torah (Genesis 46:17). The accounts vary regarding Serah's mother, with classical rabbinical literature proposing Hadurah, a descendant of Eber, as her mother. In this narrative, Asher's marriage to Hadurah is depicted as his second, with Serah's father being Hadurah's first husband. However, alternative sources, like the Book of Jubilees, present a different perspective, suggesting Asher's wife was named Ijon.

The saga of Asher and his descendants adds rich layers to the intricate narrative of the Israelite tribes, offering glimpses into their origins, blessings, and familial ties. As a pivotal character in the biblical account, Asher's legacy endures through the prosperity foretold by Jacob and the blessings bestowed upon him by Moses.

Biblical Narrative:

The Tribe of Asher is prominently featured in the Bible, with its history intertwined with the larger saga of the Israelites. In the book of Genesis, Asher is one of the twelve sons of Jacob, born to Zilpah, Leah's maidservant. The patriarch Jacob prophetically blesses Asher, envisioning his descendants as prosperous and blessed with abundance (Genesis 49:20).

As the Israelites conquer the Promised Land, the Tribe of Asher proves its mettle in battle. In the book of Joshua, Asher secures its territory and contributes to the overall success of the Israelite conquest. The Asherites' resilience and unity are celebrated as they settle into their allotted land.

In the biblical narrative found in the Book of Joshua, the division of the Promised Land among the twelve tribes follows the successful conquest of Canaan by the Israelites. According to biblical scholar Kenneth Kitchen, the generally accepted timeframe for this conquest is slightly after 1200 BC, commonly known as the 'late date,' with an alternative 'early date' placing it around 1500 BC for both the Exodus and the conquest of Canaan. However, it's crucial to note that there are dissenting views among critical scholars who argue that the described conquest in the Book of Joshua may not have taken place.

According to the biblical account, Joshua designated the western and coastal region of Galilee to the Tribe of Asher. This area, characterized by lower temperatures and abundant rainfall, boasted some of the most fertile land in Canaan, featuring rich pastures, wooded hills, and flourishing orchards. The Tribe of Asher thrived in this environment, gaining renown for its prosperity, particularly in the production of olive oil. The Blessing of Moses, found in the biblical text, seemingly prophesies this allocation, although some textual scholars consider it a postdiction.

From the time following Joshua's conquest until the establishment of the first Kingdom of Israel circa 1050 BC, the Tribe of Asher was part of a loosely connected confederation of Israelite tribes. Operating without a central government, the people were led by ad hoc leaders known as Judges during times of crisis, as depicted in the Book of Judges. In response to mounting threats from Philistine incursions, the Israelite tribes opted for a centralized monarchy, with the Tribe of Asher participating in this new kingdom under the leadership of Saul as its inaugural king (Read further in the book 'Samuel the Seer').

After Saul's demise, loyalty to the House of Saul persisted among all tribes except Judah, following Saul's son Ish-bosheth. However, upon Ish-bosheth's death, the Tribe of Asher joined other northern Israelite tribes in anointing David, then the king of Judah, as the ruler of a reunified Kingdom of Israel.

The political landscape shifted around 930 BC with the accession of Rehoboam, David's grandson. The northern tribes separated from the House of David, forming the Northern Kingdom. Asher continued its affiliation with this new kingdom until Assyria conquered its territory in 723 BC, leading to the deportation of the population. Since then, tradition has regarded the Tribe of Asher as one of the Ten Lost Tribes of Israel.

In a fascinating twist, the New Testament introduces Anna the prophetess, and her father, Phanuel, identifying them as members of the Tribe of Asher, offering a poignant connection between the Old and New Testaments.

Territory:

The tribal allotment of Asher was situated in the northwest region of Canaan, bordering the Mediterranean Sea. Its boundaries stretched from the coastal city of Tyre in the north to the plains of Acco (modern-day Acre) in the south. The lush landscape of Asher encompassed fertile plains, providing an ideal environment for agriculture and trade.

Despite its association with a general geographic region, pinning down the exact boundaries of the Tribe of Asher proves challenging when delving into the Torah. The Torah leaves room for ambiguity, raising questions about whether Asher even had a continuous and well-defined territory. The sites allocated to Asher, as outlined in the Bible and subsequently identified, present themselves as a scattered distribution of settlements rather than forming a compact and clearly outlined tribal region.

Asher's unique situation is underscored by its geographic proximity to Phoenicia, which appears to have led to a historical disconnect from the other tribes of Israel. Throughout its history, Asher seems to have remained somewhat detached from the antagonistic relationships portrayed in the Torah, such as the conflicts involving Canaanites and other Israelite tribes, as seen in the war with Barak and Sisera.

Critical scholars tend to lean towards the conclusion that Asher was comprised of specific clans affiliated with portions of the Israelite tribal confederation but never fully integrated into the broader political structure. This perspective gains further support from the fact that, along with Reuben and Gad, Asher stands out as one of the tribes for which no individual has been identified by name after the conquest. Notably, Asher and Gad are the only tribes omitted from the list of heads of tribes in I Chronicles 27, reinforcing the notion of their distinct and somewhat peripheral status within the Israelite community. The Tribe of Asher, with its elusive territorial boundaries and unique historical trajectory, adds another layer of complexity to the intricate tapestry of ancient Israelite history.

Cultural and Historical Significance:

The territory of Asher was strategically positioned, making it a hub for trade and cultural exchange. Its proximity to the Phoenician city-states, such as Tyre and Sidon, facilitated a blending of Israelite and Phoenician influences. This cross-cultural interaction likely enriched the Asherite community with diverse customs, languages, and economic opportunities.

The biblical narrative also highlights Asher's connection to the famous judge, Deborah. In the book of Judges, Asher is commended for contributing to the military efforts led by Deborah and Barak against the oppressive Canaanite king Jabin and his general Sisera (Judges 5:17).

71

Though the Tribe of Asher is not as extensively documented as some other tribes, its presence and contributions are woven into the historical fabric of ancient Israel. As with other tribes, the legacy of Asher endures through the lessons, stories, and traditions passed down through generations.

Chapter 13: The Tribe of Benjamin

The Tribe of Benjamin holds a unique and significant place within the tapestry of ancient Israelite history. From its origins as one of the twelve tribes of Israel to its role in shaping the political and religious landscape of the region, the story of Benjamin is one of resilience, triumph, and spiritual exploration. Join me as we embark on a journey through time to unravel the rich legacy of this fascinating tribe.

Origins:

Benjamin, the youngest son of Jacob and Rachel, holds a special place in the traditions of Judaism, Christianity, and Islam. His name, meaning "son of the right hand," symbolizes the favored status he held within his family. Benjamin's birth in Canaan, unlike his brother Joseph's, adds a layer of significance to his narrative.

In various religious texts, Benjamin is depicted as a righteous and favored child. The Quran refers to him as a virtuous young boy who remained with his father Jacob when his older brothers plotted against Joseph. Later rabbinic traditions even suggest that Benjamin, along with a few others, died without sin.

The origin of Benjamin's name is a subject of scholarly debate. Some believe it refers to his birthplace in Canaan, distinguishing him from his brothers born in Aram. Others interpret it as a reference to his being born in Jacob's old age. Regardless of the interpretation, Benjamin's name carries deep symbolic meaning within religious traditions.

Benjamin's role in the Joseph narrative is particularly significant. His abduction by Joseph and the subsequent test involving a silver cup serve as pivotal moments in the story. Benjamin's close relationship with Joseph is evident in

Joseph's emotional reaction upon reuniting with him, further emphasizing Benjamin's favored status.

Upon his father Jacob's death, Benjamin receives a unique blessing, likening him to a ravenous wolf, symbolizing the tribe's fierce and warlike nature, as well as its jurisdiction over the Temple in Jerusalem.

Scholars speculate about the origin of the Tribe of Benjamin, suggesting it may have been part of a larger Joseph group that migrated to Egypt and later returned to Canaan. Benjamin's sons, as listed in biblical texts, reflect his connection to Joseph and his experiences.

In Islamic tradition, Benjamin is revered as a righteous son of Jacob, born from his wife Rachel. While his narrative is less detailed in Islamic texts, the connection between Benjamin's children and Joseph is also emphasized.

Overall, Benjamin's story is one of familial love, loyalty, and divine favor. Across religious traditions, he is celebrated as a figure of virtue and significance, embodying themes of faith, perseverance, and brotherhood.

The Tribe of Benjamin's significance within Israelite society is evident throughout the Hebrew Bible. From its inclusion in the census recorded in the Book of Numbers to its role in the conquest and settlement of the Promised Land, Benjamin emerges as a key player in the unfolding drama of Israel's history.

Biblical Narrative:

During the distribution of land following the conquest of Canaan, the Tribe of Benjamin received a territory situated in the heart of the Promised Land. Its territory bordered Judah to the south and Ephraim to the north, positioning Benjamin in a strategic location within the Israelite confederation.

During the period following Joshua's conquest of the Promised Land, the Tribe of Benjamin found itself among the Israelite tribes governed by ad hoc leaders known as Judges. One of the most poignant episodes in Benjamin's narrative is the Battle of Gibeah, recounted in the Book of Judges. The tragic events surrounding the rape of a Levite's concubine led to a devastating conflict between Benjamin and the other tribes of Israel. Despite suffering significant losses, Benjamin's warriors hailed as "men of valor," displayed remarkable courage in the face of defeat.

As external threats, particularly from the Philistines, loomed large, the Israelite tribes united to form a centralized monarchy. Saul, hailing from the Tribe of Benjamin, emerged as the first king of this new entity. His reign, though marked by challenges, showcased Benjamin's pivotal role in shaping the destiny of the nascent kingdom.

Following Saul's demise, Benjamin remained loyal to the House of Saul and his successor, Ish-bosheth. However, the transition of power sparked a conflict between the House of Saul and the House of David. Negotiations between Israel's military commander, Abner, and the tribes, notably the house of Benjamin, underscored the tribe's significance in the political landscape.

After the united Kingdom of Israel dissolved, Benjamin joined the northern tribes in supporting David as king, marking a significant shift in allegiance. Despite subsequent divisions within Israel, Benjamin remained part of the southern Kingdom of Judah.

The enduring legacy of the Tribe of Benjamin is evident in its survival through tumultuous periods of Israel's history. Even after the Babylonian captivity and the loss of distinct tribal identities, echoes of Benjamin's heritage reverberate through biblical texts and historical records.

Territory:

As the Israelite tribes settled in the Promised Land, each received its portion of territory under the leadership of Joshua. While biblical accounts provide a detailed narrative of land allocation, modern scholarship offers varying perspectives on the timing and nature of the conquest.

According to tradition, Benjamin's territory stretched between Ephraim to the north and Judah to the south, with the Jordan River forming the eastern border. This land encompassed several historically significant cities, including Bethel and Gibeah, shaping Benjamin's identity within the tribal landscape.

Rabbinical sources shed light on the nuances of Benjamin's land. While specific towns on the boundary lines are named, all areas between these boundaries are considered part of Benjamin's inheritance. Cities like Lydda, Ono, and Gei Ha-ḥarashim are identified as belonging to Benjamin, reflecting the tribe's territorial extent.

Jerusalem, though allocated to Benjamin, remained under Jebusite control until King David's conquest. The city's ambiguous status within Benjamin's territory highlights the complexities of tribal boundaries and geopolitical realities.

Similarly, Bethel's ownership is subject to interpretation, with references placing it in both Benjamin and Ephraim's lands. The fluidity of territorial control underscores the intricacies of tribal history and political dynamics.

Through the ebb and flow of territorial disputes and geopolitical shifts, Benjamin's land and legacy endure. As a pivotal player in the saga of ancient Israel, Benjamin's territory serves as a testament to the tribe's resilience and enduring significance within the collective narrative of the Israelite people.

Religious and Cultural Influence:

Despite its smaller size compared to other tribes, Benjamin was renowned for its military prowess. The biblical narrative highlights the bravery and skill of Benjaminite warriors, such as King Saul, the first king of Israel, and his valiant son Jonathan. These figures played pivotal roles in defending the fledgling nation of Israel against external threats and asserting its sovereignty in the region.

In addition to its military achievements, the Tribe of Benjamin also made significant contributions to Israelite religion and culture. The city of Jerusalem, located within Benjamin's territory, became the political and religious capital of the united monarchy under King David. The construction of the Temple by Solomon further solidified Benjamin's central role in Israelite worship and spiritual life.

Legacy and Modern Perspectives:

Today, the legacy of the Tribe of Benjamin lives on through its descendants and the enduring impact of its historical contributions. While the tribe may no longer exist in its ancient form, its story continues to inspire scholars, theologians, and historians alike, offering valuable insights into the complexities of ancient Israelite society and the enduring power of faith and perseverance.

In conclusion, the Tribe of Benjamin stands as a testament to the resilience and fortitude of the Israelite people. Through triumph and tragedy, Benjamin's story reminds us of the enduring power of faith, community, and the pursuit of justice in the face of adversity. As we reflect on the legacy of Benjamin, may we draw inspiration from its rich history and continue to strive for a better future, guided by the timeless values of courage, compassion, and righteousness.

Chapter 14: The Tribe of Joseph

The Tribe of Joseph stands as a significant and multifaceted entity within the rich tapestry of ancient Israelite history. Originating from the patriarch Joseph, whose remarkable journey from slavery to prominence shaped the destiny of his descendants, this tribe encompasses two distinct branches: Ephraim and Manasseh. Through their collective narrative, the Tribe of Joseph embodies themes of providence, unity, and resilience, leaving an indelible mark on the annals of Israelite heritage.

The Tribe of Joseph, a prominent lineage among the Tribes of Israel, comprises the tribes of Ephraim and Manasseh. These two "half-tribes of Joseph" were often collectively referred to as the "tribe of Joseph." Ephraim and Manasseh were adopted by Jacob, also known as Israel, alongside his own sons, thus becoming heads of two of the twelve tribes of Israel (Genesis 48:1-16).

According to biblical accounts, Joseph, the favored son of Jacob, played a central role in the saga of the Israelite patriarchs. Sold into slavery by his brothers, Joseph rose to prominence in Egypt, eventually becoming a trusted advisor to Pharaoh and guiding the nation through a period of famine. His reconciliation with his family and subsequent adoption of his sons, Ephraim and Manasseh, into the line of inheritance, underscored Joseph's pivotal role in shaping the destiny of the tribes of Israel.

Joseph:

The biblical story of Joseph, found in the Book of Genesis, is one of intrigue, betrayal, redemption, and ultimate reconciliation. Joseph, the eleventh son of Jacob, was favored by his father, which aroused jealousy among his brothers. Their envy led them to sell Joseph into slavery, and he was taken to

Egypt, where he served in the household of Potiphar, an officer of Pharaoh.

Through a series of events, Joseph's abilities caught the attention of Pharaoh, who appointed him as a trusted advisor. Joseph's interpretation of Pharaoh's dreams—a prophecy of seven years of plenty followed by seven years of famine—proved accurate, and he was placed in charge of Egypt's grain storage during the years of abundance to prepare for the impending famine.

During the famine, Joseph's brothers journeyed to Egypt seeking food, unaware that their brother Joseph was now a powerful figure in the land. Upon their arrival, Joseph recognized them but concealed his identity. Through a series of tests, Joseph assessed his brothers' character and eventually revealed himself to them.

Joseph forgave his brothers for their betrayal and orchestrated the reunion of his family, including his aging father, Jacob, in Egypt. The story of Joseph illustrates themes of forgiveness, divine providence, and the importance of remaining steadfast in faith even in the face of adversity.

Ultimately, Joseph's story serves as a testament to the power of forgiveness and reconciliation, highlighting the transformative impact of mercy and compassion even in the most challenging circumstances.

Bibical Narrative and Teritorry:

The division of the Tribe of Joseph into Ephraim and Manasseh reflects the intricate dynamics of tribal identity and inheritance within ancient Israel. Ephraim, blessed by Jacob over his older brother Manasseh, emerged as a dominant force within the Northern Kingdom of Israel, contributing to its political and cultural landscape. Meanwhile, Manasseh, though sharing a common ancestry with Ephraim, forged its own path within the tribal confederation, navigating the complexities of territorial boundaries and historical upheavals.

Throughout the biblical narrative, the Tribe of Joseph exemplifies themes of unity and resilience in the face of adversity. From their participation in the conquest of Canaan under Joshua's leadership to their role in the establishment of the first Kingdom of Israel, Ephraim and Manasseh demonstrated a steadfast commitment to their collective heritage and destiny. Despite facing challenges such as Assyrian invasions and the eventual dispersion of the Northern Kingdom, the legacy of Joseph's descendants endures as a testament to the enduring bond between God and His chosen people.

Geographically, the territory of Joseph spanned both sides of the Jordan River. The western portion, primarily Samaria, lay between the tribes of Issachar and Benjamin. In contrast, the eastern portion extended from the Mahanaim to Mount Hermon and included the fertile lands of Bashan.

Over time, the fate of the tribe became intertwined with the northern Kingdom of Israel, leading to their eventual conquest by the Neo-Assyrian Empire and subsequent exile. Various modern-day groups claim descent from the tribe of Joseph, including the Yusufzai tribe of the Pashtuns, the Mizo Jews of Northeast India, and the Samaritans, among others. However, these claims are subject to varying levels of academic and rabbinical scrutiny.

In contemporary discussions of biblical scholarship and historical inquiry, the Tribe of Joseph remains a subject of fascination and debate. The intricate interplay of archaeological evidence, textual analysis, and theological interpretation continues to shed light on the complexities of ancient Israelite society and the enduring legacy of its tribes.

Conclusion:

In conclusion, the Tribe of Joseph occupies a central place in the mosaic of Israelite history and heritage. From its legendary origins in the patriarch Joseph to its enduring legacy within the Northern Kingdom of Israel, Ephraim and Manasseh embody the timeless themes of providence, unity, and resilience that define the Israelite narrative. As we explore the multifaceted tapestry of ancient Israel, the Tribe of Joseph stands as a testament to the enduring legacy of God's chosen people and their profound impact on the course of human history.

Chapter 15: The Tribe of Ephraim

The tribes of Israel are emblematic of a rich tapestry of history, culture, and spiritual significance. Among these tribes, Ephraim stands out prominently, noted for its pivotal role in the narrative of the Israelites. From its ancestral roots to its enduring legacy, the Tribe of Ephraim holds a unique place in biblical history.

Origins and Ancestry:

According to the Bible, the Tribe of Ephraim is descended from a man named Ephraim, who is recorded as the son of Joseph, the son of Jacob and Asenath, the daughter of Potiphera (an Ancient Egyptian woman whom Pharaoh gave to Joseph as wife). The descendants of Joseph formed two of the tribes of Israel, whereas the other sons of Jacob were the founders of one tribe each.

Ephraim's origins can be traced back to the fertile soil of Egypt, where he was born before the arrival of the Israelites from Canaan. The Book of Numbers provides insight into Ephraim's descendants, listing three sons: Shuthelah, Beker, and Tahan. However, 1 Chronicles expands upon this lineage, detailing a total of eight sons, including Ezer and Elead, whose untimely demise marked a tragic chapter in Ephraim's history.

One of Ephraim's most illustrious descendants was Joshua, the valiant leader who spearheaded the conquest of Canaan. Joshua's leadership exemplified the courage and faithfulness inherent within the tribe, as they navigated the challenges of territorial expansion and spiritual warfare.

Moreover, Ephraim's significance transcended mere genealogy, as it played a pivotal role in the establishment of the Northern Kingdom of Israel. Jeroboam, the inaugural king of this kingdom, hailed from the house of Ephraim, further solidifying the tribe's prominence in Israelite politics and governance.

Biblical scholars offer insights into the etymology of the name "Ephraim," deriving it from the Hebrew root פָּרָה (pārā), meaning "to be fruitful." This linguistic association underscores Ephraim's inherent fecundity and prosperity, symbolizing Joseph's prolificacy during his sojourn in Egypt, despite the land's afflictions.

The narrative of Ephraim and his brother Manasseh also illuminates intriguing facets of biblical interpretation. Scholars posit that originally, Ephraim and Manasseh were considered as one tribe – that of Joseph. Benjamin, another son of Jacob and Rachel, was purportedly part of this unified tribe, although this distinction became obscured over time.

Significance in Biblical Narrative:

The story of the Tribe of Ephraim is deeply intertwined with the intricate threads of biblical narrative, tracing its lineage back to its eponymous progenitor, Ephraim, the son of Joseph and Asenath. As descendants of Joseph, Ephraim and his brother Manasseh emerged as integral components of the twelve tribes of Israel, each tribe contributing to the rich tapestry of Israelite heritage.

According to biblical accounts, Ephraim's descendants played a pivotal role in the conquest of Canaan under the leadership of Joshua, a notable figure who hailed from the lineage of Ephraim himself. While biblical narratives depict the conquest of Canaan as led by Joshua, contemporary archaeological perspectives offer nuanced interpretations, viewing the Israelites as indigenous to the land, gradually developing their monotheistic faith over time.

During the era of the Judges, the Tribe of Ephraim, like other Israelite tribes, operated within a decentralized framework, characterized by ad hoc leadership and sporadic governance. However, with the escalating threat of Philistine incursions, the Israelite tribes coalesced to establish a centralized monarchy. Ephraim played a crucial role in this transition, joining the newly formed kingdom under the leadership of Saul, its inaugural king.

Following Saul's demise, Ephraim remained loyal to his house until the ascension of David, who united the divided kingdom under his rule. Yet, scholarly debates persist regarding the precise chronology of these events, challenging the traditional biblical sequence of reigns.

The zenith of Ephraim's political influence came with the reign of Jeroboam, an Ephraimite, who ascended to the throne of the Northern Kingdom of Israel. Jeroboam's reign marked a significant chapter in Ephraim's history, epitomizing its role as the embodiment of the northern tribes.

However, the glory of Ephraim was fleeting, as the kingdom eventually succumbed to Assyrian conquest in the 8th century BCE, leading to the dispersion of its inhabitants. Ephraim, along with other northern tribes, became counted among the Ten Lost Tribes of Israel, shrouded in the mists of historical obscurity.

Nevertheless, Ephraim's legacy endures, symbolizing the resilience and collective identity of the northern tribes. As a tribe that encapsulates the spirit of the Northern Kingdom, Ephraim's tale serves as a poignant reminder of the ebb and flow of ancient Israelite history, resonating with themes of unity, loyalty, and divine providence.

Territory:

In the biblical narrative, following the purported conquest of Canaan under the leadership of Joshua, the land was apportioned among the twelve tribes of Israel. While the precise dating of these events remains a subject of scholarly debate, the allocation of territories to the tribes, as depicted in the Book of Joshua, provides valuable insights into the geographical landscape of ancient Israel.

According to biblical records, the territory assigned to the Tribe of Ephraim occupied a central position within Canaan, situated west of the Jordan River, south of Manasseh's territory, and north of Benjamin's domain. This region, later known as Samaria, boasted a rugged terrain offering natural defenses and fertile soil conducive to agricultural prosperity.

The heartland of Ephraim's territory encompassed significant religious centers such as Shechem and Shiloh, which played pivotal roles in the early development of Israelite religious practices. These spiritual landmarks, coupled with the tribe's strategic location, contributed to Ephraim's prominence within the Kingdom of Israel, earning it a reputation as the preeminent tribe.

Scriptural delineations, as found in Joshua 16, outline the borders of Ephraim's inheritance in conjunction with Manasseh, providing detailed descriptions of the land apportioned to each tribe. Notably, the riverine gulch known as naḥal Ḳanah served as a natural boundary separating Ephraim's territory from that of Manasseh to the north.

The territorial extent of Ephraim stretched from the Jordan River in the east to the Mediterranean Sea in the west, encompassing a diverse array of cities and settlements. Bethel, renowned for its religious significance, featured prominently within Ephraim's domain, despite its initial allocation to the Tribe of Benjamin. Historical accounts indicate territorial disputes and realignments over time, exemplified by Abijah's military campaign to reclaim certain towns from the Northern Kingdom of Israel.

The archaeological discovery of Gezer, situated at the western fringe of Ephraim's territory, underscores the complexities of ancient territorial demarcations. While some scholars suggest Gezer marked the boundary between Ephraim, Dan, and Judah, biblical texts offer varying perspectives on the extent of Ephraim's reach to the West.

Conclusion:

The Tribe of Ephraim stands as a testament to the multifaceted nature of biblical narrative and symbolism. From its humble beginnings as a son of Joseph to its enduring legacy in prophetic literature, Ephraim's story continues to captivate and inspire seekers of spiritual truth. As we delve into the annals of history, may we glean wisdom from Ephraim's journey and strive to walk faithfully in the footsteps of our forebears.

Chapter 16: The Tribe of Manasseh

In the Israelite history, the Tribe of Manasseh emerges as a fascinating and multifaceted clan, whose legacy is woven with threads of strength, diversity, and endurance. From their origins in the biblical narrative to their enduring impact on the nation of Israel, the story of Manasseh offers a compelling glimpse into the complexities of ancient Israelite society.

Origins and Genealogy:

The origins of the Tribe of Manasseh, one of the twelve tribes of Israel, are deeply rooted in the intricate narratives of biblical history. According to Genesis 41:51, the name "Manasseh" was given to him by his father Joseph, signifying "God has made me forget entirely my troubles and my father's house." This poignant naming encapsulates the familial dynamics and the providential journey of the Israelite patriarchs.

Manasseh's lineage traces back to Joseph, the favored son of Jacob, who adopted Manasseh and his brother Ephraim to share equally in his inheritance alongside Jacob's own sons (Genesis 48:5). Despite Manasseh being the elder, Jacob chose to bless Ephraim over him, foreseeing Ephraim's descendants as surpassing his brother's. This act, conferring the blessing of the firstborn by a grandfather rather than the father, diverged from customary practices, emphasizing the significance of divine foresight and providence in shaping the destiny of the tribes.

The biblical narrative further details Manasseh's descendants, including his sons Asriel and Machir, born from both his wife and Aramean concubine, respectively (1 Chronicles 7:14). Additionally, Numbers 32:41 and Deuteronomy 3:14 mention a son named Jair, renowned for his conquests in the region of Argob, which he named Havoth Jair.

Despite being the patriarch of the tribe, the exact boundaries and relationship between Manasseh and his brother Ephraim are subjects of debate within biblical scholarship. While both tribes are described as having separate territories, they are also depicted as having enclaves within each other's lands. Moreover, textual analysis suggests that originally Ephraim and Manasseh were considered one tribe— that of Joseph. This complexity underscores the intricacies of tribal dynamics within ancient Israel, reflecting the fluidity and complexity of historical narratives.

Overall, the origins of the Tribe of Manasseh reflect the interplay of familial bonds, divine providence, and historical dynamics, shaping the identity and legacy of one of Israel's twelve tribes. Through the lens of biblical narratives, Manasseh's story serves as a testament to the enduring significance of heritage, faith, and divine guidance in the annals of Israelite history.

Territory and Inheritance:

The territorial inheritance of the Tribe of Manasseh unfolds as a complex tapestry within the biblical narratives, reflecting the nuances of ancient Israelite geography and historical dynamics. Following the purported conquest of Canaan under Joshua's leadership, the land was divided among the twelve tribes, including Manasseh.

According to the Book of Joshua, Manasseh's territory spanned both sides of the Jordan River, forming two "half-tribes" with distinct geographic features and strategic significance. In the west, West Manasseh occupied the land north of Ephraim, bordering the Jordan River and extending northwest to Mount Carmel. This region, nestled between the Jordan and the coast, boasted valuable water resources and strategic mountain passes, making it a prized possession within the Israelite confederation.

Meanwhile, East Manasseh occupied the northernmost territories east of the Jordan, stretching from Mahanaim in the south to Mount Hermon in the north. This expansive region, including the entirety of Bashan, was characterized by abundant water sources and rugged terrain, providing natural defenses and fertile lands. East Manasseh's strategic position enabled it to control vital mountain passes such as Esdraelon and Hauran, further solidifying its significance within the tribal confederation.

However, the tribe's territorial integrity faced challenges over the centuries, particularly during the tumultuous period of Assyrian invasions. In 732 BCE, Pekah, king of Israel, allied with Rezin, king of Aram, threatening Jerusalem. Ahaz, king of Judah, sought assistance from Tiglath-Pileser III, resulting in the annexation of Aram and the territories east of the Jordan, including portions of Manasseh's land. The population of these regions was deported to Assyria, marking a significant disruption to Manasseh's territorial holdings.

The riverine gulch known as naḥal Ḳanah served as a natural boundary, dividing Ephraim's territory in the south from Manasseh's in the north. Today, the modern Israeli settlement of Karnei Shomron lies near this historic gulch, serving as a tangible reminder of the ancient geographical features that shaped the tribal landscape of ancient Israel.

Characteristics and Attributes:

Throughout the biblical narrative, the Tribe of Manasseh plays a pivotal role in the unfolding saga of ancient Israel. From the time of Joshua's conquest of the Promised Land to the establishment of the first Kingdom of Israel under Saul, Manasseh remains a steadfast participant in the nation's collective journey. As part of the Northern Kingdom, Manasseh aligns with the House of Saul and later supports David's kingship, contributing to the reunification of the Kingdom of Israel. However, with the division of the kingdom under

Rehoboam, Manasseh finds itself part of the Northern Kingdom until its eventual conquest by Assyria in 723 BC.

Despite facing challenges and upheavals throughout its history, the Tribe of Manasseh endures as a symbol of resilience and continuity. Following the Assyrian conquest, Manasseh is counted among the ten lost tribes of Israel, yet its legacy lives on in the annals of Israelite history. The tribe's steadfastness in the face of adversity and its unwavering commitment to its heritage contribute to its enduring legacy, serving as a testament to the resilience of God's chosen people.

In conclusion, the Tribe of Manasseh stands as a testament to the strength, diversity, and endurance of the Israelite people. From their humble beginnings in Egypt to their prominence in the land of Canaan, the Manassehites played a pivotal role in the unfolding narrative of Israel's history. As we explore their rich heritage and enduring legacy, we gain valuable insights into the complexities of ancient Israelite society and the enduring bonds that unite God's chosen people.

Chapter 17: The Monarchy and Division

The transition from a tribal confederation to a centralized monarchy marked a significant turning point in the history of ancient Israel. This period saw the rise of powerful kings, beginning with Saul and culminating in the illustrious reign of King David. However, despite the united monarchy's initial glory, internal strife and external pressures ultimately led to the division of the kingdom into Israel (the Northern Kingdom) and Judah (the Southern Kingdom) following the reign of King Solomon.

The Rise of Monarchy:

The demand for a centralized leadership grew among the Israelites as they sought a strong and stable government to unify the disparate tribes and confront external threats. Responding to this need, Samuel, a prophet and judge, anointed Saul, a Benjamite, as the first king of Israel. Saul's reign marked the transition from a decentralized tribal confederation to a monarchy governed by a single ruler.

Under Saul's leadership, Israel experienced both victories and challenges. Despite his initial successes, Saul's disobedience to divine commands led to his downfall, paving the way for David, a shepherd and warrior, to ascend to the throne.

The Golden Age of David:

David's reign is often regarded as the golden age of ancient Israel. His military prowess, political acumen, and devotion to God solidified his rule and expanded Israel's territory to its greatest extent. David's victories over neighboring enemies, such as the Philistines and the Ammonites, established Israel as a dominant regional power.

In addition to his military achievements, David is celebrated for his contributions to Israel's spiritual and cultural life. He established Jerusalem as the capital city and brought the Ark of the Covenant into the city, symbolizing God's presence among his people. David's psalms, poetic expressions of faith and devotion, continue to inspire believers to this day.

The Division of the Kingdom:

Despite the glory of David's reign, his legacy was marred by internal strife and familial conflict. Following his death, his son Solomon succeeded him as king. While Solomon's reign was marked by prosperity and grandeur, his heavy taxation and forced labor alienated many of his subjects, leading to discontent and rebellion.

After Solomon's death, the kingdom faced a succession crisis, with his son Rehoboam inheriting the throne. In response to the people's grievances, the northern tribes, led by Jeroboam, rebelled against Rehoboam's rule, establishing the Kingdom of Israel with its capital in Samaria. Meanwhile, Rehoboam retained control over the southern tribes, forming the Kingdom of Judah with Jerusalem as its capital.

Conclusion:

The transition from tribal confederation to monarchy, under the leadership of Saul and David, brought both triumphs and tribulations to ancient Israel. While the united monarchy reached its zenith under David's reign, internal divisions and external pressures eventually led to the kingdom's split into Israel and Judah. Despite this division, the legacies of Saul, David, and Solomon endure as foundational figures in the history and identity of the Israelite people.

Chapter 18: Exile and Diaspora

The Assyrian and Babylonian exiles stand as watershed moments in the history of ancient Israel, marking periods of profound upheaval and dispersion for the Israelite tribes. These events shattered the unity of the nation, scattering its people across distant lands and challenging their ability to maintain tribal identity and cohesion.

The Assyrian Exile:

In the 8th century BCE, the mighty Assyrian Empire launched a series of military campaigns against the northern kingdom of Israel. In 722 BCE, after a prolonged siege, the capital city of Samaria fell to the Assyrian forces, and the kingdom of Israel was conquered. The Assyrians deported a significant portion of the Israelite population, dispersing them among the various provinces of the empire.

For the exiled Israelites, life in Assyria presented numerous challenges. Separated from their homeland and communities, they faced the daunting task of preserving their cultural and religious identity amidst foreign surroundings. While some assimilated into Assyrian society, others clung tenaciously to their ancestral customs, language, and faith, striving to maintain a sense of unity and cohesion.

The Babylonian Exile:

The Babylonian Exile, occurring in the 6th century BCE, had an equally profound impact on the Israelite people. In 586 BCE, the Babylonian king Nebuchadnezzar II besieged Jerusalem, destroying the city and its temple and deporting a significant portion of the population to Babylon. This event, known as the Babylonian Captivity, marked the end of the kingdom of Judah and the beginning of a period of exile for the Jewish people.

During their time in Babylon, the exiled Israelites faced similar challenges to those of their northern counterparts. They grappled with questions of identity, community, and faith in the midst of a foreign land. Yet, despite the hardships, the Babylonian exile also became a period of cultural and spiritual renewal for the Jewish people. It was during this time that they began to codify their religious texts, preserving and interpreting their sacred traditions for future generations.

Maintaining Tribal Identity in Exile:

The challenge of maintaining tribal identity and cohesion in exile was multifaceted. The loss of ancestral land, the disruption of communal life, and the imposition of foreign customs all threatened to erode the distinctiveness of the Israelite tribes. Yet, even in exile, the bonds of kinship, shared history, and common faith served as anchors for the dispersed communities.

Efforts to preserve tribal identity took various forms, including the continued observance of religious rituals and festivals, the transmission of oral traditions and genealogies, and the establishment of communal structures and institutions. Leaders emerged within the exilic communities, providing guidance, spiritual leadership, and a sense of unity in the face of adversity.

Conclusion:

The Assyrian and Babylonian exiles represented periods of immense upheaval and dispersion for the Israelite tribes. Yet, amidst the challenges of exile, the Israelite people demonstrated resilience, adaptability, and a fierce determination to preserve their tribal identity and heritage. These experiences laid the groundwork for the emergence of the Jewish diaspora, shaping the history and destiny of the Israelite people for centuries to come.

Chapter 19: What Tribe of Israel Did You Descend From?

Now that we have discussed the history of Jacob and the origins of each of the twelve tribes, let's talk about you.

If you are Jewish, you are a descendent of those bloodlines, but can you tell which one? Let us try and explore what tribe of Israel did *you* descend from.

The short answer to the question is probably Judah, as most Jews are descended from it. If your family name is either Levy/Levi or one of its abbreviations, then you can be traced back to the Kohanim (Priests) or Levites, which means you descend from the tribe of Levi. And there are other unique cases we specify below, referring to the 10 other "lost tribes" that were exiled from the land of Israel after being conquered by Assyria.

Within ancient Judaism, one's tribal affiliation had a great impact on his or her practices and opportunities, as some tribes enjoyed privileges others did not and some tribes received more blessings than others. On the other hand, some modern scholars dispute whether there ever were (exactly) twelve Israelite tribes, and think that the number 12 more likely signifies a symbolic invented tradition as part of a national founding myth.

For the most part, tribal identities have been lost through the generations, and the majority of Jews do not know which tribe they are from. It is believed that most living Jews are descendants of Judah and its allied tribes (Benjamin, Dan, Shimon). However, there are some exceptions.

<u>**Tribe of Levi:**</u>

There are a number of people whose families have passed down their identity as Kohanim (Priests) or Levites, which means they descend from the tribe of Levi.

The surnames that can be traced to this tribe are either Levy/Levi or one of its abbreviations: Levine or Segal (Hebrew abbreviation for "Segen" – meaning Levy) – or one of the priestly names (Levy was the priestly tribe) such as Cohen, Kagan (Russian pronunciation of Cohen), Kaplan (German corruption of Capella), Katz (Cohen-Tzedek – righteous priest).

Other Tribes:

There are also a handful of non-Levite families who can trace their ancestry to a particular tribe, but these are few and far between.

As we mentioned before, only two tribes survived when the Kingdom of Israel was destroyed. That was Judah (which is why we are called Jews) and Benjamin. Having said that, members of other tribes had survived when they escaped the Assyrians or were living in the south (with Judah and Benjamin). Those are called "the lost 10 tribes" and can be traced to different locations.

The Tribe of Reuben – Reuben was a member of the Northern Kingdom of Israel until the kingdom was conquered by Assyria. The tribe of Reuben at this time was no longer recognizable as a separate force in this area. Even if still present at the outbreak of this war, the outcome of this war would have left them without a territory of their own, just like the tribes of Simeon and Levi.

The Tribe of Simeon – An apocryphal midrash claims that the tribe was deported by the Babylonians to the Kingdom of Aksum (in what is now Ethiopia), to a place behind the dark mountains.

The Tribes of Ephraim and Manassah – As part of the Kingdom of Israel, the territories of Ephraim and Manassah were conquered by the Assyrians, and the tribes were exiled. the manner of their exile led to their further history being lost. However, several modern-day groups claim descent, with varying levels of academic and rabbinical support. The Samaritans claim that some of their adherents are descended from this tribe, and many Persian Jews claim to be descendants of Ephraim. Further afield, in India, the Telugu Jews claim descent from Ephraim and call themselves Bene Ephraim, relating similar traditions to those of the Mizo Jews, whom the modern state of Israel regards as descendants of Manasseh.

The Tribe of Issachar – Remains from the tribes of Ephraim, Manasseh, Issachar, and Zebulun stayed in the territory of Judah after the exile of the ten tribes in the Babylonian Exile.

The Tribe of Zebulun – As part of the Kingdom of Israel, the territory of Zebulun was conquered by the Assyrians, and the tribe was exiled. the manner of their exile led to their further history being lost.

The Tribes of Dan, Gad, Asher, and Naphtali – Ethiopian Jews, also known as Beta Israel, claim descent from the Tribe of Dan, whose members migrated south along with members of the tribes of Gad, Asher, and Naphtali, into the Kingdom of Kush (now Ethiopia and Sudan), during the destruction of the First Temple. As noted above the Tribe of Simon was also deported to the Kingdom of Aksum (in what is now Ethiopia).

Speaking from a purely scientific point of view, there is no real way to know which tribe of Israel one descend from, and it is even not that clear if those twelve tribes actually existed. As the believers say, when the Messiah comes, we will all find out which tribes we are from. So if this bit of information is important to you, do your best to hasten his arrival.

Chapter 20: The Tribes of Jesus, Mary, Joseph, and Other Gospel Figures

The Bible, particularly the New Testament, holds within its pages rich narratives that trace the ancestry and lineage of Jesus Christ, as well as other pivotal figures in the Gospel accounts. Understanding the tribal origins of these figures offers profound insights into their cultural context and spiritual significance. In this exploration, we delve into the tribes of Israel from which Jesus, Mary, Joseph, and other prominent figures hailed, as revealed through biblical texts and historical context.

Jesus of Nazareth:

The lineage of Jesus Christ is meticulously documented in the Gospels of Matthew and Luke. Both accounts trace his ancestry through different lineages, emphasizing different aspects of his heritage. Matthew's Gospel highlights Jesus' connection to the royal line of David, crucial for establishing his messianic credentials. Meanwhile, Luke's Gospel provides a broader genealogy, tracing Jesus' lineage all the way back to Adam, underscoring his universal significance.

In terms of tribal affiliation, Jesus is traditionally associated with the tribe of Judah. This connection is crucial because the Messiah was prophesied to come from the tribe of Judah, as seen in Genesis 49:10:

"The scepter will not depart from Judah, nor the ruler's staff from between his feet, until he to whom it belongs shall come and the obedience of the nations shall be his."
Genesis 49:10

A glance back at Jesus genealogy confirms this at Luke 3:33:

"son of Am·min'a·dab,
son of Ar'ni,

son of Hez'ron,
son of Pe'rez,
son of Judah,"
Luke 3:33

Mary, the Mother of Jesus:

While the New Testament does not explicitly state Mary's tribal affiliation, early Christian tradition has often linked her lineage to the tribe of Judah as well. This association is derived from her genealogy provided in the Gospel of Luke, where she is depicted as a descendant of King David. Since David was of the tribe of Judah, Mary's lineage is presumed to be from the same tribe.

Joseph, the Husband of Mary:

Joseph, the earthly father of Jesus, is traditionally regarded as being from the tribe of Judah. However, there are no explicit biblical references confirming Joseph's tribal lineage. Some scholars suggest that Joseph's ancestry might have been a mixture of different tribes, given the intermingling of tribes over generations.

John the Baptist:

John the Baptist, Jesus' cousin and precursor, is described in the Gospels as being from the priestly line of Aaron. His father, Zechariah, served as a priest in the Temple, indicating John's affiliation with the tribe of Levi. The Gospel of Luke portrays John as a direct descendant of Aaron, emphasizing his role as a priestly figure preparing the way for the Messiah.

Epilogue

As we conclude our journey through the rich tapestry of ancient Israelite history, we are left with a profound sense of awe and admiration for the resilience, faith, and enduring legacy of these tribes.

From the earliest days of tribal confederation to the heights of monarchy under King David and the division of the kingdom, the Israelites faced numerous trials and triumphs. They weathered internal conflicts, external threats, and the challenges of exile and diaspora, yet they never lost their sense of identity or their connection to their ancestral homeland.

Despite the dispersion of the tribes and the passage of millennia, the spirit of ancient Israel lives on. Its influence can be felt in the faith traditions of Judaism, Christianity, and Islam, as well as in the enduring impact of its cultural and literary heritage.

As we reflect on the story of ancient Israel, let us remember the lessons it teaches us about resilience, faith, and the enduring power of community. May we draw inspiration from the trials and triumphs of the Israelite tribes as we navigate our own journeys through history. And may we always remember the legacy of ancient Israel, which continues to shape the world to this day.

Further Resources:

Thank you for embarking on this journey through the captivating history of ancient Israel with us.

As we conclude this book, we invite you to continue exploring the fascinating world of ancient civilizations and beyond. Visit our website for further reading, resources, and insights into the diverse cultures and histories that have shaped our world.

We are grateful for your interest and support, and we hope that the knowledge gained from this journey will continue to inspire and inform your understanding of the past, present, and future.

With warm regards,

www.IsraelByLocals.com